Thomas Viskum Gjelstrup Bredahl

Adherence to physial activity

Psychological aspects in Prescribed Exercise and Motivational counselling

LAP LAMBERT Academic Publishing

Impressum/Imprint (nur für Deutschland/only for Germany)
Bibliografische Information der Deutschen Nationalbibliothek: Die Deutsche Nationalbibliothek verzeichnet diese Publikation in der Deutschen Nationalbibliografie; detaillierte bibliografische Daten sind im Internet über http://dnb.d-nb.de abrufbar.
Alle in diesem Buch genannten Marken und Produktnamen unterliegen warenzeichen-, marken- oder patentrechtlichem Schutz bzw. sind Warenzeichen oder eingetragene Warenzeichen der jeweiligen Inhaber. Die Wiedergabe von Marken, Produktnamen, Gebrauchsnamen, Handelsnamen, Warenbezeichnungen u.s.w. in diesem Werk berechtigt auch ohne besondere Kennzeichnung nicht zu der Annahme, dass solche Namen im Sinne der Warenzeichen- und Markenschutzgesetzgebung als frei zu betrachten wären und daher von jedermann benutzt werden dürften.

Coverbild: www.ingimage.com

Verlag: LAP LAMBERT Academic Publishing GmbH & Co. KG
Dudweiler Landstr. 99, 66123 Saarbrücken, Deutschland
Telefon +49 681 3720-310, Telefax +49 681 3720-3109
Email: info@lap-publishing.com

Approved by: Odense, University of Southern Denmark, Diss., 2010

Herstellung in Deutschland:
Schaltungsdienst Lange o.H.G., Berlin
Books on Demand GmbH, Norderstedt
Reha GmbH, Saarbrücken
Amazon Distribution GmbH, Leipzig
ISBN: 978-3-8465-1137-4

Imprint (only for USA, GB)
Bibliographic information published by the Deutsche Nationalbibliothek: The Deutsche Nationalbibliothek lists this publication in the Deutsche Nationalbibliografie; detailed bibliographic data are available in the Internet at http://dnb.d-nb.de.
Any brand names and product names mentioned in this book are subject to trademark, brand or patent protection and are trademarks or registered trademarks of their respective holders. The use of brand names, product names, common names, trade names, product descriptions etc. even without a particular marking in this works is in no way to be construed to mean that such names may be regarded as unrestricted in respect of trademark and brand protection legislation and could thus be used by anyone.

Cover image: www.ingimage.com

Publisher: LAP LAMBERT Academic Publishing GmbH & Co. KG
Dudweiler Landstr. 99, 66123 Saarbrücken, Germany
Phone +49 681 3720-310, Fax +49 681 3720-3109
Email: info@lap-publishing.com

Printed in the U.S.A.
Printed in the U.K. by (see last page)
ISBN: 978-3-8465-1137-4

Preface

The evaluation of *Exercise on Prescription* was initiated and completed in collaboration with Funen County and Frederiksberg Municipality, Denmark. This thesis is based on the evaluation carried out during my enrolment as a PhD student at the Faculty of Health Sciences, University of Southern Denmark. The study was approved by the Danish Data Protection Agency 2005-41-5248, and registered with ClinicalTrials.gov ID NCT00594360. Due to the non-biological and non-treating perspective of the study no registration to the local ethics committee was needed. The Study was funded by the Faculty of Health Sciences, University of Southern Denmark, the National Board of Health, Denmark, Funen County and Frederiksberg Municipality.

Acknowledgements

I would like to thank everybody who helped me during my work with the thesis; in particular I would like to thank:

Kirsten Kaya Roessler and Lis Puggaard for inspiring supervision and cooperation during the thesis.

John Singhammer for statistical assistance

Kirsten Kjær for technical assistance

Kristoffer Henriksen, Jes Bak Sørensen, Arne Gårn and Anne Rossel for contributing to the on-going process of the project.

The Exercise on Prescription participants from Funen County and Frederiksberg Municipality for their contribution to the project.

My colleagues at the research group of psychology, and at the Institute of Sports Science and Clinical Biomechanics.

My family and friends for their interest and support throughout the project.

I would like to dedicate this PhD thesis to my wife Birgitte and my wonderful children Jeppe, Mie and Mathilde.

Odense, May 2010

Thomas Viskum Gjelstrup Bredahl

Table of Contents

Table of contents

Abbreviations and definitions

Anamnesis	A statement of the history and development of a disease on the basis of the patient's or the environment's information and experiences
BMI	Body Mass Index, weight/height^2 (kg/cm^2)
CI	Confidence interval
DF	Degrees of Freedom
Emergens	This concept describes how the whole of a system is more than the sum of the parts in the same system
EoP	Exercise on Prescription, the concept of prescribing exercise in primary healthcare
Exercise	The performance of some activity in order to develop or maintain physical fitness and/or overall health
Exercise specialist	A person educated in sports science and health and responsible for planning and implementing exercise and giving motivational counselling
GP	General Practitioner
MET	Estimation of energy expenditure measured as metabolic equivalents (kcal/kg×h).
Modern diseases	Modern diseases are in this context defined as e.g. fibromyalgia and whiplash syndrome
Physical activity	Bodily movement produced by the contraction of skeletal muscles resulting in energy expenditure. A wider term than exercise including activities performed with no objective or an objective completely different from that of exercise (e.g. walking as transportation)
PG	Prevention Group, the group receiving motivational counselling only

Prescriped Exercise	The concept of prescribing exercise in primary healthcare
SD	Standard Deviation
SE	Standard Error
Self-efficacy	Confidence in one´s ability to conduct a given task or behaviour is strongly related to one´s ability to perform that behaviour
Social relations	The individuals key contact persons (e.g. family, friends, GP, exercise specialist, and other participants)
Stages of change	Individuals changing behaviour move through the stages precontemplation, contemplation, preparation, action, and maintenance in their effort to change behaviour
Training	Planned behaviour for developing specific skills or muscles
TG	Treatment Group, the group receiving supervised training as well as motivational counselling

Introduction

This thesis is a compilation of four published papers, with considerable overlap between the thesis and these papers. Nevertheless, the thesis includes additional material, hypotheses and analyses which are not included in the papers.

A sedentary lifestyle is related to an increased risk of lifestyle diseases, e.g., cardiovascular disease, high blood pressure, and type 2 diabetes (Haskell et al., 2007; Lindstrom et al., 2006; Pedersen & Saltin, 2006). The risk of these lifestyle diseases decreases with an increased level of physical activity (Andersen et al., 2000) and aerobic fitness (Blair et al., 1996). Physical activity is recommended as a treatment for, as well as to prevent, a number of lifestyle diseases (Haskell et al., 2007; Pedersen, 2003; Pedersen & Saltin, 2006). Despite growing knowledge concerning the benefits of physical activity, an increasing number of people are finding it difficult to meet the recommended amount of health beneficial physical activity (WHO, 2004). Approximately half of the Danish population is not sufficiently active (Willeman, 2004) and studies show the same tendency for the American population (Fenton, 2005; van Sluijs, 2004; Yancey et al., 2004). This high proportion of inactive people is posing a serious threat to public health (WHO/FAO, 2003).

Interventions have been created to support the increasing demands for physically active lifestyles. In many countries (e.g., New Zealand, Great Britain, Sweden and Denmark), *prescribed exercise* is used to facilitate physical activity in sedentary populations with, or at risk of developing, lifestyle diseases (Elley et al., 2003; Harrison et al., 2005b; Sorensen et al., 2007). Different methods have been used to promote physical activity, such as oral advice from a general practitioner (GP), phone-based counselling (Elley et al., 2003) and oral counselling from an exercise specialist (Aittasalo et al., 2006). Studies of this type of intervention show varied results. Some studies indicate a positive effect on specific lifestyle diseases (Roessler & Ibsen, 2009; Tuomilehto et al., 2001; Whelton et al., 2002), but other studies suggest that *prescribed exercise* has a moderately positive (Sorensen et al., 2006) or no (Hillsdon et al., 2005) effect on physical activity level. Furthermore, researchers question the effect of exercise prescriptions on a population level (Harrison et al., 2005a). Yet, this kind of intervention is still widely used to promote physical activity (Dugdill et al., 2005). In essence, a large proportion of participants stop being physically active after intervention even though the aim and future perspective are adherence with a physical active lifestyle.

Some proportion of the limited effect of physical activity and *prescribed exercise* interventions could possibly be ascribed to a treatment tradition bound in the established biomedical paradigm. Traditionally, biomedical treatment has been used to treat lifestyle diseases, without focussing on behavioural change and possible underlying psychological and social factors (Agger, 1991; Elsass, 2000; White, 2005). Thus, since long-term effects and adherence to physical activity interventions and *prescribed exercise* to some degree fail to happen (Harland et al., 1999; Harrison et al., 2005b; Jones et al., 2005; Taylor & Fox, 2005), it is necessary to include other holistic or psychological and practical perspectives when developing physical activity programmes and *prescribed exercise* interventions.

As an example of a holistic approach, health psychological theories emphasise the fact that behaviour change is anchored in a psychological, social and physiological context (Antonovsky, 1979; Biddle & Fox, 1998; Elsass et al., 2004). The importance of the interaction between these factors is underlined by health psychology research, which shows that these factors in combination influence the individual's health status and ability and will to change behaviour (Bandura, 1986; Biddle & Nigg, 2000; De Vries et al., 1998; Fox et al., 1997; Prochaska & Diclemente, 1983; Roessler & Ibsen, 2009). Based on previous research showing a moderate (Elley et al., 2003; Fleming & Godwin, 2008; Roessler & Ibsen, 2009; Sorensen et al., 2006) or minimal effect (Hillsdon et al., 2005; Sorensen et al., 2008) of *prescribed exercise*, it is essential that attention be directed towards psychological and social issues as well as the physiological, if the creation of successful prescribed physical activity interventions aiming at behaviour change are wanted (Biddle & Fox, 1998).

To expand the present biomedical paradigm towards a more integrative and holistic paradigm, the next section of the thesis describes the historical development of the biomedical treatment paradigm and discusses the difficulty of using this paradigm to treat newer and more complex diseases and illnesses. Furthermore, the section includes a discussion of the need for a bio-psycho-social approach to accommodate these issues. Moreover, in concordance with the above-mentioned need to enhance the treatment effect of *prescribed exercise* interventions, the use of a bio-psycho-social approach to influence long-term behaviour change is discussed.

Theoretical background

A health-psychological perspective

The history of the biomedical paradigm

In modern Western society, it is common for people to contact a General Practitioner (GP) for cases of uneasiness, discomfort, disease or illness (Elsass, 2000; Elsass et al., 2004; Elsass & Lauritsen, 2006; Kleinman, 1988). Following this initial contact, the GP examines the individual for possible physical indications of disease. If the GP cannot locate any indications or the diagnosis is unclear, the individual is often referred to a medical specialist or is sometimes sent home with a message from the GP saying the symptoms are not definable from the GP's educational and paradigmatic context. The medical specialist holds further competence to analyse the individual's state of health. The individual is analysed from the perspective that a biomedical explanation can be found (Tinetti & Fried, 2004). In the area of biomedicine, biological causes of disease are pursued to find the best possible treatment using agents with a pharmacological character. This fundamental biological way of seeing illness is tied to a biomedical paradigm, with roots reaching far back in history (Dewalt & Pincus, 2003; Winau, 1990).

From humoralpathology to biomedicine

The humoralpathology, as one of the first medical concepts, was developed by the Greek physician Galenos. He gathered and systematised medical knowledge in the 2nd century. The humoralpathology was founded upon a model addressing the balance between earthly elements and bodily fluids. This balance is derived from a state of equilibrium between the four elements of water, earth, fire and air. If the individual balance between the elements is maintained, the individual stays healthy; but should an imbalance occur, illness or disease will emerge. This way of regarding health and disease remained a dominant concept of disease for almost 2000 years (Engelhardt, 2001; Sjostrand, 2002).

One of the first more consistent attempts to develop a new medical concept occurred in the Middle Ages. At this time, a scholastic, marked dogmatism dominated in general, in which diagnostics and treatment were limited to the examination of bodily fluids, without further knowledge of bodily anatomy and composition. These methods of examination constituted a foundation for diagnosis as well as treatment. Due to this, the anatomical body played no significant role for the medical diagnosis. This form of diagnostics was used as late as the 18th century, despite the still dominating humoralpathology (Marx, 1992; Winau, 1990).

In the 15th century, the Dutch physician Vesal tried to challenge the concepts of Galenos. He revealed the Galenic anatomy as the anatomy of animals and challenged it by his own newly developed anatomical analysis of the human body. Vesal's attempt to challenge the humoralpathology created the basis for the study of human anatomy, which turned into a new science (Paweletz, 2001). As a consequence of this, the human body was discovered in its whole and afterwards in detail (Marx, 1992; Paweletz, 2001; Webster, 1993). Vesal formed a new paradigm through anatomy and his knowledge of the body. However, the concept of biomedicine remained divided – the increasing knowledge of the human body gained ground, while the concept of disease, still founded in the humoralpathology, remained unchanged (Winau, 1990).

Around the same time Vesal was focussing on the human body, Paracelsus, who was a professor in medicine, presented an Iatrochemical[1] theory, in which alchemy constituted a central position (Engelhardt, 2001; Webster, 1993). Paracelsus opposed the Galenic way of thinking (Webster, 1993). The Iatrochemical theory was developed into a science that examined the chemical composition and the function of the human body. The treatment of the patient changed and came to include treatment with chemical substances. The aim was to lead to a stabilisation of the chemical state of equilibrium in the body and thereby generate recovery (Engelhardt, 2001; Webster, 1993; Winau, 1990). Iatrophysics[2] developed afterwards as yet another challenge to the humoralpathology. In this paradigm, the body is considered a machine, functioning according to physical and mechanical laws. Still, Iatrophysics had, as did Iatrochemistry, difficulty breaking the monopoly of the still dominating humoralpathology (Benini & Deleo, 1999; Winau, 1990).

The first actual decisive break from humoralpathology came in 1761, when Italian professor of anatomy Morgagni argued that diseases could be causally lead back to organ changes (Balint et al., 2006). The conception of the body as a morphological whole was now dissolved. This change lead to the acceptance of the fact that the body as a whole no longer was considered ill and the concept of disease changed character to primarily focus on organ changes as the basis for disease. The result

---

[1] A medical theory of the 16th and 17th centuries, which argued that biological processes were chemically determined (Milner, 1996; Webster, 1993).
[2] A medical theory of the 17th and 18th centuries that argued that diseases and processes in the body were determined by physical and mechanical laws. These could be affected by physical and mechanical means (Milner, 1996).

of this localisation of diseases was that the unity of the body as a whole to a great extent was lost (Winau, 1990).

Against this background, the German pathologist and physician Virchow introduced the theory of cellular pathology[3] in the middle of the 19th century (Brown & Fee, 2006; Dewalt & Pincus, 2003). This medical concept had decisive impact on the biomedical conception of the body and created the framework for an Iatrotechnical theory of disease. This theory proposes that the human body is divided into organs, tissue, cells and functions, through which the localisation and anatomical residedence of diseases is related to the smallest organic unit possible (Brown & Fee, 2006; Dewalt & Pincus, 2003). Therefore, disease was often considered a malfunctioning in a machine and the body was reduced, further than it was in Cartesian dualism, to a mechanical functioning connection of individual parts (Benini & Deleo, 1999; Winau, 1990). This view was based upon Descartes' dualistic conception, wherein the body and soul are considered to be independent and to have different properties. In the second part of the 19th century, this concept of disease, with its focus directed towards the physiology of the body, resulted in a *biomedical paradigm* that did not leave room for feelings and thoughts, as these were considered to be a part of the soul (Dewalt & Pincus, 2003).

In the early 1900s, the Austrian physician and psychoanalyst Sigmund Freud developed his psychoanalytic paradigm. Freud was a pioneer in his field, and his work introduced the possibility of conducting scientific experiments on the mind and the unconscious. The background for his working method, as is also current in the biomedical sciences, was observation of the psychological system in isolation. Freud's treatment of the psychological aspects as medical phenomena thus supported the dualism started by the Cartesian split (Uexküll, 1996).

In 1928, Alexander Flemming introduced penicillin (Flemming, 1980; Goldsworthy & McFarlane, 2002). The later developed antibiotics and sulphate compounds of the 1940s allowed extraordinary treatment effects of until then untreatable diseases, such as pneumonia and other infectious diseases (Bennett & Chung, 2001). This development entailed to a considerable degree the physicians' confidence in pharmacology and treatment on a cellular level. Disease was considered a physiological disturbance, which could be corrected or brought to order by the right pharmacological treatment. New scientific fields, such as biochemistry, microbiology,

---

[3] A biomedical paradigm which considers the cell as the carrier of diseases (Brown & Fee, 2006; Winau, 1990).

pharmacology, immunology and genetics, whose areas of interest were isolated parts of the body, were developed. The Western medical concept thus was formed. The unity, i.e., the individual and his/her disease, was analysed, understood and treated on the basis of single parts (Engel, 1977; Engel, 1997). In summary, the historical development of the biomedical paradigm can be described as a development from humoralpathology, which represents the whole person in balance or imbalance, as well as the whole body, to a biomedical orientation that splits the body and soul, in which the individual as a whole loses his/her value. A division was created consisting of a somatic biomedicine, which only focuses on sick bodies without souls, and a psychological medicine, which solely focuses on sick minds without bodies (Agger, 1991; Elsass, 2000; Elsass et al., 2004; Tinetti & Fried, 2004).

The biomedical model

This historical development and specialisation changed the physician's way of studying the patient. Conversation, anamnesis[4] and information about the patient's experiences were de-emphasised. Instead, contact between the GP and patient is centred on a collection of various clinical and laboratory factors. This clinical practice is built upon, among other things, the following fundamental assumptions: a) scientific rationality, b) objective, quantitative measures, c) biochemical data, d) dualism and the division of body and mind, e) the hypothesis that diseases constitute isolated units and f) an emphasis on the specific patient instead of the environment (Elsass, 2000).

In treatment, prevention, compliance and adherence, the consultation between the physician and the individual should be considered very important (Elsass, 2000). The individual meets the physician with his/her own story of discomfort or illness. This discomfort or illness, during the consultation and because of the physician's paradigm and educational background, often is reshaped into a diagnosis and an objective disease or defined as not being a disease (box 1) (Elsass, 2000; Elsass et al., 2004; Engel, 1977).

---

[4] A statement of the history and development of a disease on the basis of the patient's information and experiences (Milner, 1996).

Illness and disease

The concepts of illness and disease refer to the physician's rephrasing of the individual's own understanding of discomfort. Illness constitutes a unifying concept for the popular conception of symptoms and complaints and is the "living experience" of bodily processes. The experiences relate to the life story of the individual as well as unique illness experiences. These experiences for example are shaped by culture (Kleinman, 1988; Uexküll, 1996). Disease characterises the professional physician's conception and originates from the physician's socialisation within the biomedical paradigm. As an example, the individual's problems are expressed in biological terms which fit the biomedical model. This leads to a description of the condition as changes in the individual's biological functioning (Elsass, 2000; Elsass et al., 2004; Kleinman, 1988).

Box 1. The definition of illness and disease.

One explanation for the reshaping could be that some of the experiences the individual describes are insignificant and consequently unnecessary for the clinical diagnosis. But via this reshaping, essential parts of the illness experience are at risk of being lost (Elsass, 2000; Elsass et al., 2004). This is unfortunate, because the potential problems enclosed in the illness experience can be of great importance to the individual and can be a symptom of different undesirable conditions in the individual environment. This is also problematic, because somatic diseases can have a psychological background and mental illnesses can be accompanied by somatic side effects (Agger, 1991; Elsass, 2000; Elsass & Lauritsen, 2006; Tinetti & Fried, 2004; White, 2005). Disease and illness behaviour therefore can also be explained from the social and psychological contexts in which the symptoms occur (Kleinman, 1988). This is supported by the WHO definition of health from 1948, which states that health is "a state of complete physical, mental and social well-being and not merely the absence of disease or infirmity" (WHO, 1948; WHO, 2009). This means that practitioners who work within this classic biomedical structure often can and will overlook information of significance for patients' treatment (Elsass, 2000; Tinetti & Fried, 2004; White, 2005). This is happening despite research showing psychological and social conditions as important in terms of their possible impact on the development of a disease (Ader & Cohen, 1993; Cohen et al., 1997; Elsass, 2000; Rabin et al., 1989; Rabin, 1999; Uchino et al., 1996). The physicians' professional knowledge and abilities should be able to encompass social as well as cultural, psychological and biological issues to ensure high quality treatment for individual patients (Elsass, 2000; Elsass et al., 2004; Engel, 1977; Tinetti & Fried, 2004; White, 2005).

13

From biomedicine to a bio-psycho-social model

Within the last thirty to forty years, patients who are treated within the present biomedical paradigm express discontent to a greater degree than earlier (Tinetti & Fried, 2004; Uexküll, 1996; White, 2005). A reason for this can be that diseases over time have changed character from infection related diseases to diseases of civilisation (Agger, 1991; Elsass et al., 2004). These diseases, e.g., cardiovascular diseases and cancer, are characterised as lifestyle diseases which primarily occur due to individual ways of living. In spite of increased treatment efforts within this area, the results have lacked efficiency in curing diseases. One of the explanations for this inefficiency might be a possible change in the complexity of diseases (Christensen, 1988; Christensen & Sommer, 2002). This change is illustrated in the figure below, showing three major waves of disease in the 19th century (figure 1).

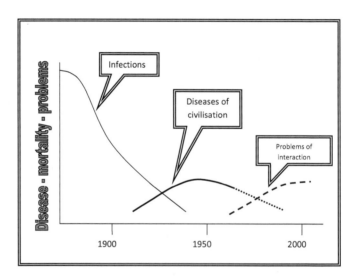

Figure 1: The three major waves of disease in the 19th century (translated from Christensen, 1988, p. 249).

According to this model, "diseases of civilisation" should be extended by diseases as emerging on the basis of problems with interaction and communication with the environment. The individuals reactions to disease should be considered a part of an interaction, a social intercourse and a collaboration between the individual and his/her environment (Roessler, 2002; Tinetti & Fried, 2004; Uexküll, 1996; VanLeeuwen et al., 1999). Thus, a disease should be considered an expression

14

of an individual's conditions of life and an expression of the life the individual leads (Christensen, 1988). Hence, the way the individual leads his/her life is not only determined by his/her lifestyle, but is also influenced by the environment and the framework in which the individual lives (Elsass, 2000; Engel, 1992; Uexküll, 1996).

This consideration underscores the need for a new theoretical model, as the biomedical model does not encompass psychosocial factors to a satisfactory level, but to a great degree considers disease from an individual perspective. Support for a revised medical model is apparent in the table below, which illustrates that in some areas regarding the individual's health there are different ways of defining disease (table 1).

The percentage who wanted to give a notification of illness	General practitioners	General population
1. Chronic back pain	50%	84%
2. Acute back pain	42%	53%
3. Recurrent back pain	49%	81%
4. Chronic neck-shoulder pain	49%	54%
5. Neck-shoulder pain and social problems	26%	25%
6. Whiplash syndrome	80%	92%
7. Fibromyalgia	49%	54%
8. Depression	58%	38%
9. Acute grief after death of spouse	38%	42%
10. Exhaustion because of demented spouse	13%	40%
11. Pneumonia	100%	93%
12. Cold without fever	12%	7%
Number of participants	194	321

Table 1. The evaluation of twelve anamneses in two selected groups. The proportion of the general practitioners and the general population, who wanted to give a notification of illness to the specific patient (translated from Iversen, 2002, p. 30).

The information presented in the table suggests that general practitioners and patients to some degree experience diseases or illnesses in different ways. Chronic back pain is considered a severe health problem for 84 percent of the general population, while only 50 percent of the GPs consider it a disease. The same issue is apparent with recurrent back pain and exhaustion because of demented spouse (Iversen, 2002). The illnesses not categorised within specific measurable areas, such as many pain syndromes, are therefore not diagnosed as diseases. This emphasises that the methods used to determine an individual's diagnosis have become obsolete in relation to new patterns of diseases[5] (Christensen, 1988; Iversen, 2002). These new patterns of disease, and the differences between physicians' and patients' conceptions of illnesses, provide further strong

---

[5] New patterns of diseases in this context are defined as, e.g., fibromyalgia, chronic pain and whiplash syndrome (Iversen, 2002).

evidence of the need for a new medical model (Elsass et al., 2004; Engel, 1992; Engel, 1997; Uexküll, 1996; VanLeeuwen et al., 1999).

The bio-psycho-social model

In acknowledgement of the inadequacy of the biomedical paradigm, recent decades have experienced an expansion of the existing model towards a bio-psycho-social model (Roessler, 2002; Tinetti & Fried, 2004; Uexküll, 1996; VanLeeuwen et al., 1999).

One of the first attempts to broaden the biomedical model, by developing a bio-psycho-social approach, has historical roots in the theoretical discussions of Engel (1977), who from his position as professor of psychiatry tried to develop a possible replacement for the biomedical model. He developed a model based on the Systems Theory (Engel, 1977; Engel, 1982). His theory was built upon a hierarchical model that included the individual and his/her surroundings (figure 2). Every level in the hierarchy represents an organised dynamic whole and because of this contains a certain amount of important information. Every unit in the system is affected by and is affecting the other units in the system.

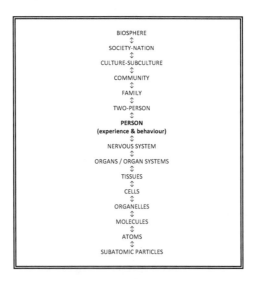

Figure 2: Hierarchy of Natural Systems (from Engel, 1982, p. 803).

The figure illustrates that it is possible, at any given point in time, to study all levels, within the sphere of the individual, involved in the development of a disease. The knowledge gained from this way of analysing illness or disease could make it possible to intervene at the correct time-point and at the correct level. Seen from Engel's perspective, the Systems Theory worked as a basis for a new bio-psycho-social model, which could be used by several professions within the medical sciences (Engel, 1977; Engel, 1982).

German professor of medicine Thure Von Uexküll elaborated further on Engel's model, and developed the concept "emergens". Emergens describes how the whole of a system is more than the sum of its parts. Within this system, new qualities, not explainable from the single units' qualities, emerge (Uexküll, 1996). According to the concept of emergens, signals from the environment are always interpreted by the individual's psychological system, which entails that an unconscious mechanism leads to conscious actions. Because of this individualised interpretation, mechanical reactions alone to physical changes are not possible. Hence, this argues additionally for an integrative model of understanding illness and disease which includes psychological and social issues as well as biological (Uexküll, 1996).

In a Danish context, a further development of Engel's and Uexküll's theories, and the interaction between biological, social and psychological aspects and between the individual and the environment, are described by Iversen (2002). The individual is considered an active part in actively forming his/her environment, and reacts actively to illness or disease (Iversen, 2002). An example of an expanded bio-psycho-social model that seeks to combine these complex relations is illustrated in figure 3 below.

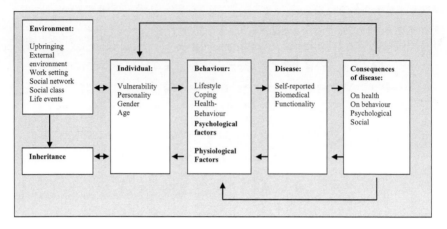

Figure 3: Bio-psycho-social model of causes to and consequences of disease (translated from Iversen, 2002, p. 40).

According to this model, the individual is a product of inheritance and existing conditions in childhood, but also in present life. Interactions between the individual and environmental factors, such as, upbringing, social network and life events, are of importance. These factors characterise, e.g., the individual's vulnerability and personality and influence to what degree the individual can and will adopt a given behaviour (Engel, 1997; Iversen, 2002; Roessler, 2002; White, 2005). In some cases, the individual adopts a behaviour that leads to illness or disease. The consequences of the illness or disease directly or indirectly affect the individual via physiological as well as psychological and environmental factors and thereby form a circular pattern of interaction (Lutgendorf & Costanzo, 2003). This pattern of mutual interaction is confirmed by research in the area of psychoneuroimmunology (Ader & Cohen, 1993; Cohen et al., 1997; Rabin et al., 1989; Rabin, 1999; Zachariae, 1996). Consequently, these interactions between the individual, the environment and behaviour play an important role for health and, furthermore, for a possible adoption of health enhancing behaviours (Elsass, 2000; Elsass et al., 2004; Iversen, 2002; Lutgendorf & Costanzo, 2003; Thing, 2005).

Another model developed in a Danish context illustrates the above-mentioned interaction between physical, psychological and social factors in a sport and exercise context (figure 4) (Roessler, 2002). This model shows in a distinct way the circular and mutual impact of physical, psychological and social factors. In an exercise activity or sports context, following interactional patterns can be existing; for example, can high expectations of an athlete combined with group pressure from a team lead to overtraining resulting in a fatigue fracture. In this example, psychological aspects start the interaction process. But an injury can also be the starting point of a process that can lead to social isolation and later depression (Roessler, 2002).

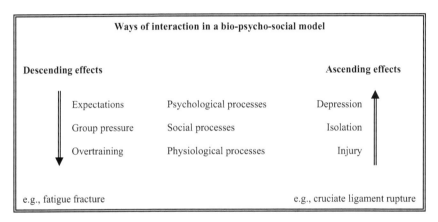

Figure 4: Ways of interaction in the bio-psycho-social model (translated from Roessler, 2002, p. 13)

In summary, the above-mentioned theoretical perspectives and integrative models show that it is meaningless merely to take an isolated look at individuals' somatic, psychological and social problems and try to solve these separately. The complex relationship which is present regarding these problems has to be recognised. Interactions between physical factors, individual interpretations and the surrounding environment should be taken into account in a multi-factorial context when trying to understand, analyse or influence illness, disease or behavioural change (Roessler, 2002; Tinetti & Fried, 2004; Uexküll, 1996; VanLeeuwen et al., 1999; White, 2005).

The bio-psycho-social model, lifestyle and behaviour change

As argued in the previous section, diseases, lifestyles and behaviours can be understood from different perspectives. Even though some theorists argue for using and integrating a bio-psycho-social approach in the treatment and prevention of lifestyle diseases, thereby influencing behaviours, the majority of today's lifestyle interventions are organised in a fashion that still reflects the domination of the traditional biomedical approach (Christensen & Albertsen, 2002). Paradigms differ regarding how to interpret the concept of lifestyle and this difference is apparent in the organisation of lifestyle interventions attempting to influence health and exercise behaviours (e.g., Exercise on Prescription).

According to the traditional biomedical understanding of lifestyle, in regards to behaviour, the focus is on the individual's responsibility for his/her own life and health. This individualisation emphasises that the individual is responsible for his/her own actions, life and health. In this sense, lifestyle is interpreted as a narrow term related to specific and selected health behaviours (e.g., exercise behaviour) (Biddle & Fox, 1998; Skovgaard, 2004). For example, healthy eating and physical activity typically have been understood solely as individually determined physiological factors, thereby disregarding possible sensuous values of the different activities (Johannessen, 2005). From a biomedical perspective, it is logical to emphasise the responsibility of the individual for staying healthy and physically active, and consequently to design individualised interventions (Johannessen, 2005). However, studies implementing interventions on an individual level in relation to lifestyle, health and physical activity behaviours have not shown substantial changes in regards to health promotion and behaviour change. Furthermore, research on health, behaviour and lifestyle has shown that a narrow conception of lifestyle is not useful for trying to understand and influence individual lifestyles and health behaviours (Johannessen, 2005). Broader conceptions of lifestyle and health are needed (Jensen, 2009). To increase the impact of interventions and better understand the minimal effect of biomedical behaviour interventions on health, the social sciences offer a more complex understanding of lifestyles and health behaviours which might be useful to employ. Moreover, it is important to use this understanding to supplement the already existing knowledge from the biomedical tradition, to gain a better understanding of behaviour change (Almind & Hansen, 2009).

Research from the social sciences indicates that behaviour is not an individualised matter, but instead is an integrated part of the individual's social life, influenced by other central factors within the individual's context (Eichberg, 1993; Johannessen, 2005; Ottesen, 1993). The social sciences

20

suggest, as does the bio-psycho-social model, it is important to recognise that lifestyle and health behaviours are influenced by a large number of factors, which the individual can influence only to a limited degree (Christensen & Albertsen, 2002). Within the social sciences lifestyle has been used to describe, e.g., consumption habits, choice of cultural activities and health-related habits across the social classes (Christensen & Albertsen, 2002). Figure 5 depicts how individual health behaviour is influenced not only by intentional effort of the individual, but also by conditions of life (in Danish "levevilkår"), way of life (in Danish "livsformer") and lifestyle (Eichberg, 1993; Johannessen, 2005; Ottesen, 1993) (figure 5). Here, lifestyle is defined by the society and the culture (e.g., environment, legislation, material resources) in which the individual lives, the local environment (e.g., work, family, social relations, economic resources), the individual's preconditions (e.g., gender, life-events, psychological characteristics) and, furthermore, the possibilities and limitations which the current situation encompasses (Johannessen, 2005). The individual interpretation of these factors determines lifestyle and thereby health-related behaviours (e.g., physical activity behaviour) (Antonovsky, 2000; Due & Holstein, 2009; Lazarus & Folkman, 1984; Uexküll, 1996).

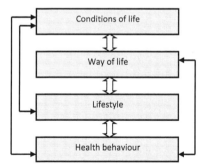

Figure 5. An example of the relationship between conditions of life (in Danish "Levevilkår"), way of life (in Danish "Livsformer"), lifestyle and health behaviour (composited of Eichberg, 1993; Johannessen, 2005; Ottesen, 1993).

The individual lives and acts out his/her lifestyle(s) within a given context (Eichberg, 1993), and health behaviour (e.g., physical activity behaviour) is a narrower concept which includes the habits and activities that influence the individual's health (Due & Holstein, 2009). Lifestyle has typically been used to describe behavioural patterns in groups of people, whereas health behaviour predominantly has been used to describe individual behaviour and actions. In conclusion, lifestyle as well as health behaviour include intentional, deliberate and customised actions that influence health (Christensen & Albertsen, 2002; Due & Holstein, 2009).

Thus, it could be argued that an individual does not have a specific lifestyle and health behaviour for conscious and deliberate reasons alone, but these are the result of a combination of several factors (Thing, 2005; Thing, 2007). It is apparent from research that it is reasonably easy to affect individuals' physical activities as long as interventions are ongoing, but very difficult to maintain once interventions have stopped (Sherwood et al., 2008). Therefore, as also argued in relation to the bio-psycho-social model, it is important in regards to interventions, lifestyle and behaviour to include and sustain the dynamics of the multi-factorial relationships among physiological, psychological, social and cultural dimensions in order to understand and influence individual health behaviours (Iversen, 2002; Jensen, 2009; Johannessen, 2005; Thing, 2005).

A variety of methodologies can be used to explore the complexity of health behaviour. A systemic or holistic study, which includes numerous factors and approaches from different sciences, can qualify the approach to explore the complexity of health behaviour. Such a study could provide an overview of the coherence between factors, and interactions between the individual and the environment, but requires complex research methodologies, teams of researchers and vast resources.

Collecting data from multi-disciplinary studies is another approach. In a multi-disciplinary study, research from different sciences or branches of sciences provides information regarding the same subject, thus providing an overview (Jorgensen et al., 2000). This methodology could provide valuable knowledge concerning different areas of Exercise on Prescription, but not necessarily contribute with knowledge of coherence between these areas or help determine how the whole of a system can be more than the sum of its parts (Uexküll, 1996).

In the current thesis, lifestyle and physical activity behaviour are analysed using a multi-disciplinary approach. Earlier research has already determined the physiological effect of *prescribed exercise* (Harrison et al., 2005a; Hillsdon et al., 2005), and an adjusted Health Technology Assessment (HTA) (Bredahl et al., 2010) has been used in a Danish setting to analyse the training (Roessler & Ibsen, 2009; Sorensen et al., 2008), the organisation (Andreassen, 2007; Skovgaard et al., 2009) and the economical factors (Bredahl et al., 2010) of Exercise on Prescription. The current thesis on physical activity and behavioural change aims to supplement already existing knowledge with health psychological aspects of Exercise on Prescription in Funen County and Frederiksberg Municipality.

Acknowledging that lifestyle and physical activity behaviour should be understood in a broader biological, social, environmental and cultural context, the choice to focus on specific psychological and social areas place the theoretical focus of this thesis in a more established tradition of health research, where behaviour change is considered more of an individual responsibility. The psychological and social areas concerning physical activity and behaviour change in Exercise on Prescription are in this thesis primarily analysed as an individual matter, thereby somewhat disregarding the established complexity of lifestyle and behaviour. This theoretical focus has been chosen to supplement the already existing knowledge (training, organisation and economy) concerning Exercise on Prescription, with a health psychological analysis and thereby contribute to a multi-disciplinary (but not systemic) understanding of Exercise on Prescription and its effect on physical activity behaviour. Moreover, the theoretical focus was chosen due to an already existing and comprehensive research paradigm providing a theoretical basis, methodological discussions and developed methodology. Even though this approach does not accommodate a systemic and holistic analysis of individuals trying to adapt to a physically active lifestyle, compiled knowledge from multi-disciplinary analyses will provide valuable knowledge on Exercise on Prescription.

The following sections of "Exercise and Health psychology" will provide a selected overview of the above-mentioned research paradigm that has provided the source for the individual psychological focus of this thesis.

Health Psychology and exercise

Physical Activity and Behaviour Change

In sports science, researchers have adopted theories and models from general, social, educational, and health psychology and tested and applied them in the context of physical activity behaviour, primarily with an individual focus (Sutton, 2004). Biddle and Nigg attempt to organise and systematise key theoretical frameworks into a classification system (Biddle & Nigg, 2000, p. 292) (figure 6). The authors point out that their model is to be understood as heuristic, and there is overlap between categories (Biddle & Nigg, 2000). In general, theories of exercise behaviour can be divided into five categories: beliefs and attitudes, perception of competence, perceptions of control, stage-based theories and hybrid approaches.

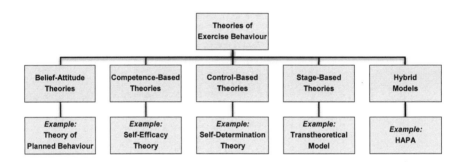

Figure 6. A framework for classifying theories of physical activity (Adapted from Biddle & Nigg, 2000, p. 292)

Belief-Attitude Theories

Belief-attitude theories examine the links between beliefs, attitudes, intention and physical activity. Attitude has been one of the most applied and influential constructs in social psychology and has been incorporated into many approaches for understanding physical activity behaviour (Biddle et al., 2007). An example of this is the Theory of Reasoned Action (TRA) or the later developed Theory of Planned Behaviour (TPB) (Ajzen, 1991; Ajzen & Fishbein, 1980). In TRA, intention indicates the degree of planning and effort people are willing to invest in their performance of future behaviours. Both cognitive change theories predict that the more favourable an individual's attitude and subjective norm, the stronger his or her intentions are to perform the behaviour (Biddle et al., 2007). One reason for the wide use of attitude as a predictor of physical activity is the presumption that attitude predicts behaviour. Research indicates that the model has reasonable support for predicting physical activity and exercise intentions. In addition, attitudes appear to be stronger predictors of physical activity than are social norms (Biddle et al., 2007). However, a gap between attitude, intention and behaviour has often been reported (Hagger et al., 2002). Research within this area needs greater emphasis on how to translate attitude and intentions into behaviour (Biddle & Mutrie, 2007). One criticism of the TPB is that it is a unidirectional model which predicts behaviour from measures of behavioural intention measured at one point in time. Furthermore, the model solely relies on cognitions and thereby omits other potentially important determinants of action, such as environmental influences. Moreover, the TPB investigates the interrelationships between constructs of the model and a single behaviour. It does not account for alternative behaviours (Biddle & Mutrie, 2007).

Competence-Based Theories

The Self-efficacy theory is included among competence-based theories (Bandura, 1986) and has been extensively used with research studying individual motivation in exercise psychology (Biddle & Nigg, 2000). The construct *self-efficacy* has been documented as one of the most consistent predictors of physical activity behaviour. *Self-efficacy* is defined by Bandura as:

> *Peoples' judgements of their capabilities to organize and execute courses of action required to attain designated types of performances. It is concerned not with the skills one possesses, but rather with judgements of what one can do with whatever skills one possesses. (Bandura, 1986, p. 391)*

The Self-efficacy theory states that confidence in one's ability to conduct a given task or behaviour is strongly related to one's ability to perform that behaviour (Bandura, 1986). *Self-efficacy* beliefs are closely bound to the accomplishment of behaviour, such as physical activity and exercise (Sallis et al., 1986). Bandura suggests that the strength of *self-efficacy* is influenced by prior successes or performance attainment, imitation and modelling of people similar to oneself, verbal and social persuasion, and judgements of psychological states The framework this theory offers has had a great impact on exercise and health research (Biddle et al., 2007; McAuley & Blissmer, 2000). The individual's confidence has been indicated as an important factor in exercise motivation. Statements made by research participants concerning self-perceptions of confidence regarding physical activity or sport in research have been found to be associated with the initiation or maintenance of physical activity (McAuley et al., 2003; McAuley & Blissmer, 2000). Research concerning non-patient exercise groups has indicated that a high *self-efficacy* expectation regarding physical activity can predict exercise participation, especially in the early stages of an exercise programme (McAuley et al., 1994). Additionally, research has shown that *self-efficacy* can be increased through intervention, such as participating in physical activity, and that this increase again can positively influence physical activity participation (Biddle & Mutrie, 2007). The level of *self-efficacy* can be understood both as a cause of an increased level of physical activity, but also as an effect of participation (Biddle & Mutrie, 2007; Marshall & Biddle, 2001; McAuley et al., 1994; McAuley et al., 2003). Consequently, studies of *self-efficacy* and exercise behaviour are needed to investigate how *self-efficacy* influences and is influenced across other physical activity or exercise settings. Furthermore, an assessment of *self-efficacy* needs to be associated with other factors, such as e.g. potential barriers (Biddle et al., 2007).

Control-Based Theories

Research incorporating Control-based theories indicates that changes in exercise behaviour are associated with a need to control the lifestyle and that perceptions of control are important for health-related behaviours at the individual level (Hagger & Chatzisarantis, 2007). The Self-Determination Theory (SDT) (Deci & Ryan, 1991) is a popular theory of human motivation in exercise and sport psychology. The theory is built upon earlier work concerning intrinsic and extrinsic motivation (Biddle & Nigg, 2000; Vallerand, 2007). It is related to three basic psychological needs: competence, autonomy and relatedness (Chatzisarantis & Hagger, 2007). SDT uses control and competence to explain individual exercise behaviour and focuses on the need to experience oneself as an initiator and regulator of one's actions (Deci & Ryan, 1991). The context surrounding the individual is considered to be chaotic if the environment is unstructured and significant others do not provide any feedback (Deci & Ryan, 1991). The interpersonal context is considered supportive when significant others encourage behaviour and acknowledge feelings and perspectives (Hagger & Chatzisarantis, 2007). Competence, autonomy and relatedness can contribute to predicting how and in which circumstances intrinsic motivation can be promoted (Biddle & Mutrie, 2007; Vallerand, 2007).

Stage-Based Theories

The theories presented earlier consider changes in behaviour to be primarily continuous, where behaviour change is due to developmental progress. In this section stage-based theories, which assume that the development of health behaviour happens within qualitatively different stages are presented. The best-known and widely used stage-based model is the Transtheoretical Model (TTM), often referred to as the *stages of change* framework (Biddle et al., 2007; Biddle & Nigg, 2000). The Transtheoretical Model was developed by Prochaska and Diclemente (1983) to describe different stages involved in changing and maintaining behaviour. The model suggests individuals change behaviour through the stages of Precontemplation (no intention to change behaviour), Contemplation (intention to change behaviour), Preparation (preparing to change behaviour), Action (currently changing behaviour) and Maintenance (sustaining behaviour change). The progression through stages is thought to be dynamic, with individuals progressing through stages at various rates, with some individuals getting stuck at certain stages and others relapsing to previous stages (Marcus & Simkin, 1994; Prochaska & Diclemente, 1983). The amount of progress individuals make as a result of an intervention is a result of the stage they were in when the intervention was initiated (Jones et al., 2005). The model of the *stages of change* states that behaviour change is dynamic and individuals who stop performing a specific behaviour may intend to start again (Marcus et al., 1992b).

Other constructs included in the Transtheoretical Model, in addition to *stages of change*, are Processes of Change, Decisional Balance and *Self-efficacy*. Processes of Change are defined as the cognitive, affective and behavioural strategies and techniques people use when they pass through the different *stages of change* over time (Marcus et al., 1992a). Processes of Change are hypothesised to increase in a linear fashion up to the stage of action and to level off during the maintenance stage (Biddle & Mutrie, 2007), but a meta-analysis has indicated that Processes of Change additionally increase from precontemplation to contemplation and from preparation to action (Marshall & Biddle, 2001). Decisional Balance suggests that during the change process people continuously weigh the advantages of change against the disadvantages of change. Research indicates that disadvantages outweigh advantages in the early stages of a change process, whereas individuals who are in the maintenance stage perceive more advantages than disadvantages (Marshall & Biddle, 2001). *Self-efficacy* (as described above) has also consistently been shown to increase with progress in *stages of change* (Marshall & Biddle, 2001).

The TTM has received a great deal of attention from researchers and has been used in exercise and physical activity interventions (Biddle & Nigg, 2000). The model is appealing because it provides researchers and practitioners with concrete strategies on how to intervene in each stage (Biddle & Nigg, 2000; Prochaska & Diclemente, 1983). Research has shown that it is useful to include different stages of readiness for change as a framework for understanding behaviour and behaviour change (Biddle et al., 2007; Biddle & Mutrie, 2007; Marshall & Biddle, 2001). This success in health settings indicates it would be an appropriate application for physical activity behaviour. The majority of studies using TTM in analyses of physical activity and exercise behaviour have used the model in cross-sectional analysis (Marshall & Biddle, 2001). The need for longitudinal analyses using the TTM as a framework is thus clear.

Hybrid Models

The Health Action Process Approach (HAPA) is a model that explicitly tries to integrate continuous and stage models (Biddle et al., 2007; Schwarzer, 1992) (figure 7). The HAPA illustrates the distinction between a motivation phase and a post-decision phase of health behaviour. When the individual moves from a motivational phase to a volitional phase, a shift in perception is experienced. The HAPA model illustrates three phases. In the "non intentional phase", a behavioural intention is being developed under the influence of, e.g., risks, decisional balance and *self-efficacy*. Next, the individual enters the "intentional phase", when the intention has already been formed, but the individual remains inactive while behaviour is being planned or prepared. In this phase, *self-efficacy* is important, especially if barriers occur. The individual then enters the "action phase" if the desired behaviour is initiated. In this phase, *self-efficacy* is still an important factor for influencing the maintenance of behaviour. The HAPA also incorporates factors such as barriers and resources (Biddle et al., 2007; Biddle & Mutrie, 2007; Schwarzer, 1992).

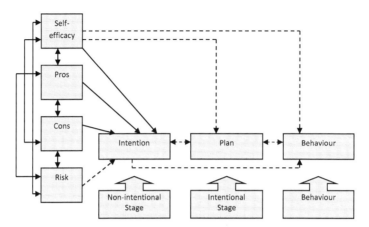

Figure 7. The health action approach (HAPA). Dashed arrows indicate stage-specific effects and mechanisms. Solid arrows indicate generic effects (Adapted from Biddle et al., 2007, p. 552; and Schwarzer, 1992, p. 233).

Most of the theories presented in this section focus on individual psychological processes, but environmental factors are also important in these models (Biddle & Mutrie, 2007). For example, the Theory of Planned Behaviour includes "normative beliefs" and external regulation, which is defined as the interaction between individuals. Furthermore, the Self-determination Theory includes extrinsic forms of motivation.

In summary, the models presented here have been used to a great degree in research on exercise behaviour, but in particular the *Self-efficacy* Theory and the Transtheoretical Model have been used extensively (Biddle et al., 2007; Biddle & Nigg, 2000). These empirically supported models have been shown to be applicable for creating interventions that help people move from one stage to the next. They have offered practitioners the possibility of designing programmes and treatments that are more efficient and effective than interventions in which all individuals are offered the same treatment (Biddle et al., 2007). Therefore, to improve treatment interventions, it is important to transfer knowledge from evaluations and research into practice.

Physical activity behaviour, stages of change, self-efficacy and social relations

The overview of psychological models that focus on behaviour change and physical activity presented in the previous section, "Physical Activity and Behaviour Change", illustrates that the Transtheoretical model, which incorporates the construct of *self-efficacy*, is one of the most extensively used in research concerning physical activity and behaviour change. Moreover, Exercise on Prescription (EoP) is an intervention that has implemented research findings associated with these theories in the organisation of the intervention and in motivational counselling, as described in the section "Exercise on Prescription in Funen County and Frederiksberg Municipality". The motivational counselling in EoP is structured on the principles of Motivational Interviewing (Miller & Rollnick, 2002). Furthermore, the principles of Motivational Interviewing are founded upon research on *self-efficacy* and *stages of change*.

Self-efficacy and *stages of change* are incorporated in the analyses of individual psychological factors important for changes in EoP participants because of the thorough research on *self-efficacy*, *stages of change* and adoption of physical activity behaviour, and furthermore, because they are an integral part of Exercise on Prescription.

A combination of the approaches of *self-efficacy* (Bandura, 1986), *stages of change* (Prochaska & Diclemente, 1983) and social relations (Biddle et al., 2007; Biddle & Nigg, 2000; Iversen, 2002) elucidate important psychological factors influencing behaviour change (Biddle & Mutrie, 2007; De Vries, 1988; De Vries, 1998; Jackson et al., 2003; Marshall & Biddle, 2001; Sallis et al., 1989; van Sluijs, 2004).

Stages of Change elucidates to what extent the individual is ready to make a given change (Prochaska & Diclemente, 1983; van Sluijs et al., 2004). Researchers debate this issue and conflicting results are apparent (Adams & White, 2005). Some studies (Adams & White, 2003) indicate an effect of stage-based interventions, whereas others indicate little or no effect of stage-based interventions (van Sluijs et al., 2004; van Sluijs et al., 2005b). Despite the conflicting results, it could be relevant for the Danish version of Exercise on Prescription to clarify whether the participant's placement in the stages (i.e., a) precontemplation, b) contemplation, c) preparation, d) action, and e) maintenance) is positively influenced during the intervention or to what extent this influences long-term adherence to physical activity.

Self-efficacy, referring to the individual evaluation of the possibility of regulating a given behaviour or action, is dependent on abilities and individual expectations of mastering specific actions. *Self-efficacy* also refers to conquering general barriers in an effort to change major or minor parts of a habitual lifestyle to achieve a desired goal (Bandura, 1986; Bandura, 1995; Bandura, 1997). As noted earlier, *self-efficacy* has been identified as a stable predictor for changes in exercise behaviour. The level of *self-efficacy* prior to and during a physical activity intervention is shown to influence physical activity adherence in the early and middle stages of an intervention (Biddle et al., 2007; Marshall & Biddle, 2001; McAuley et al., 2003). Therefore, it is important to study *self-efficacy* both as a cause and an effect in relation to EoP and the individual's barriers, which could possibly stand in the way of converting intention into action or physical inactivity into physical activity (Bandura, 1997; Bess, 1992; Holm et al., 2003).

Social relations are defined as relationships between individuals. They are characterised by complex conditions and have been shown to have great impact on individual behaviour and have come into focus within psychosocial health research (Andersen, 1998; Lund & Due, 2002). Research shows that both the quantity and quality of social relations can affect an individual's health and behaviour (Cohen et al., 1997; Iversen, 2002; Uchino et al., 1996). For example, social relationships can act as facilitators in regards to physical activity behaviour, but they can also directly affect individual health behaviour through positive or negative role models (Ajzen & Fishbein, 1980; Hagger et al., 2002; Lund & Due, 2002). Social support is often considered a one-dimensional concept without regarding the complexity of the social relations. Often, the various quantitative and qualitative dimensions of social relationships are not taken into account. The fact that social relations do not necessarily act as support, and thus do not affect an individual's health in a positive direction, is often not taken into consideration. If the concept is instead considered as multidimensional, a more nuanced picture of possible supportive but also stressful relationships will appear (Hagger et al., 2002; Uchino et al., 1996; Yalom, 1985). Research has shown social relations to have important impact on behaviour and change in regards to, e.g., lifestyle diseases and exercise (Biddle & Mutrie, 2007; Bolman & De Vries, 1998; Trost et al., 2002; Yalom, 1985). It is relevant to investigate to what extent and how central psychosocial areas (in this thesis defined as family and friends, general practitioners, physiotherapists, exercise instructors, exercise specialists, places of exercise and other participants) contribute to maintaining or improving a participant's adherence to physical activity (Willeman, 2004).

31

Overall, psychological factors, social networks and their effect on behaviour are addressed in this thesis. Integrated in the bio-psycho-social model of Iversen (2002), the highlighted areas in figure 8 are the focus of the current thesis (figure 8).

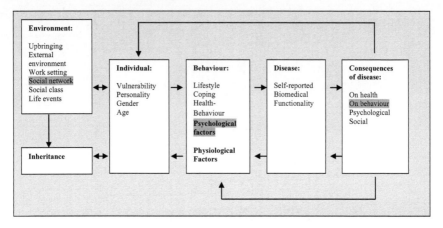

Figure 8. Bio-psycho-social model of causes to and consequences of disease (translated from Iversen, 2002, p. 40). Highlighted areas illustrate the areas that are addressed in the thesis.

Exercise on Prescription

Exercise on Prescription – the Danish initiative

The Danish government published in 2002 a health programme aiming at increasing life expectancy and quality of life (Regeringen, 2002). Physical inactivity is mentioned as a main area of focus. To increase the number of physically active people interventions and/or initiatives should include: general information, target group information, counselling, and physical activity as part of treatment and rehabilitation (Regeringen, 2002). Exercise on Prescription (EoP) is an example of an intervention aiming at behaviour change by increasing physical activity and thereby reducing symptoms from lifestyle diseases. The National Board of Health recommended and supported EoP-interventions, but initiatives were organised and implemented by the Counties and Municipalities. Due to the local administration and organisation of EoP by Counties and Municipalities the design of the interventions differed to some extent.

The EoP scheme or developed models of EoP was widely used in e.g. Municipalities to increase physical activity amongst sedentary individuals with or in risk of developing lifestyle diseases. Only a few studies in Denmark have evaluated the effect of EoP in regards to physiological outcome showing moderate (Roessler & Ibsen, 2009) little or no effect (Sorensen et al., 2008) and limited knowledge exists about the impact of EoP on the patient perspective (Roessler & Ibsen, 2009; Sorensen et al., 2006; Sorensen et al., 2008). A new report from the Danish National Board of Health concludes EoP offers developmental potential (Bredahl et al., 2010) and a PhD thesis from 2008 emphasises the patient perspective as an important area for future research to improve new EoP interventions (Sørensen, 2008).

Exercise on Prescription in Funen County and Frederiksberg Municipality

This section describes how the EoP intervention was organised by Funen County and Frederiksberg Municipality. The EoP intervention was divided into two central parts, which included a high-intensity general EoP treatment scheme as well as a lower-intensity prevention scheme of "Motivational counselling". In this thesis, the two forms of intervention will be referred to as the Treatment Group (TG) and the Prevention Group (PG). The intervention design for the TG and the PG in Funen County and Frederiksberg Municipality was organised as shown in figure 9.

Inclusion criteria

The TG was directed towards individuals with specific medically controlled lifestyle diseases. The GPs could refer sedentary individuals with medically controlled and diagnosed lifestyle diseases known to be affected by physical activity (e.g., type 2 diabetes and cardiovascular diseases) (Pedersen, 2005; Pedersen, 2003; Sundhedsstyrelsen, 2004; Sundhedsstyrelsen, 2006). An internal report, from Region Syddanmark (Hea, 2008), describing research on a sample of 100 participants, estimates the percentage of different lifestyle diseases included in the TG by the GP in Funen County, as illustrated in table 2. Data from Frederiksberg Municipality were not available, but a fairly similar report of Exercise on Prescription in Copenhagen, with 1622 participants (Roessler et al., 2007), indicates the percentage of different lifestyle diseases, as illustrated in table 2. The table illustrates that participants with primarily three lifestyle diagnoses are included in the interventions: type-2 diabetes, hypertension and dyslipidemia. Furthermore, it is apparent that a great proportion of the participants are diagnosed with more than one lifestyle disease.

Lifestyle Disease	Funen County (%)	Copenhagen Municipality (%)
Type-2 Diabetes (T2D)	18	10
Hypertension	47	21
Dyslipidemia	10	18
Ischaemic heart disease	4	----
T2D + Hypertension	15	9
T2D + Dyslipidemia	----	8
Dyslipidemia + hypertension	2	21
T2D + Hypertension + Dyslipidemia	----	12
Other diagnoses	5	1

Table 2. Percentage of lifestyle diseases included in the EoP in Funen County (n = 100) and Copenhagen Municipality (n = 1622) (Hea, 2008; Roessler et al., 2007).

The individuals should be motivated to change lifestyle (this was estimated through personal conversation) and should believe to be able to improve health from an increased level of physical activity. They should also be willing to pay 750 Dkr. (100 €) for the intervention (Sorensen et al., 2007). After referral to the TG, about half of the patients receiving a prescription contacted the physiotherapist or the exercise specialist to schedule an initial appointment to join the TG.

The PG was directed towards healthy citizens at risk of developing lifestyle diseases (e.g., type 2 diabetes and cardiovascular diseases) due to physical inactivity. Since the PG participants were not diagnosed with lifestyle diseases, but only at risk of developing one, no percentages or distributions of lifestyle diseases were available. At the GP the participant could be advised to join PG by their general practitioner if they were physically inactive and/or did not meet any medically controlled condition to be enrolled in the TG. Furthermore, the participants could be enrolled by their own initiative by directly contacting the physiotherapist or exercise specialist. The physiotherapist or exercise specialist decided whether the participant met the inclusion criteria. Information about the PG was available at pharmacies, local media and health organisations (e.g. Diabetes Society, Heart Society, and The Danish Cancer Society). The participants in the PG entered the intervention by their own initiative.

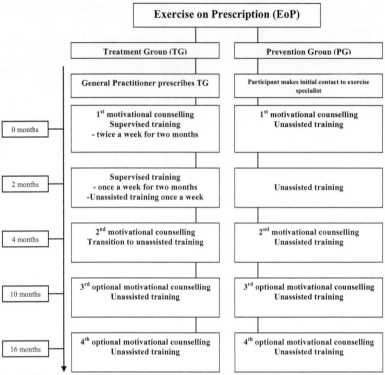

Figure 9. Schematic overview of Exercise on Prescription in Funen County and Frederiksberg Municipality
Schematic overview of the two groups: The Treatment Group (TG) and the Prevention Group (PG) in
Exercise on Prescription. In the TG the general practitioner (GP) prescribes Exercise on Prescription for
sedentary individuals with medically controlled conditions. The individual takes the prescription to a
physiotherapist or an Exercise Specialist working with Exercise on Prescription. The participants complete
four months of supervised training and motivational counselling. In the PG the participant contacts the
physiotherapist or Exercise Specialist working with Exercise on Prescription. The participants are included
to the PG if they are sedentary and in risk of developing lifestyle diseases that can be positively influenced
by physical activity. The participants carry out unassisted exercise and receive motivational counselling at 0,
4, 10 and 16 months.

Training and motivational counselling

The participants in the TG followed a supervised group-based training intervention along with 8-12 other TG participants (including participants not taking part in the study). The group-based supervised training was carried out by physiotherapists or exercise specialists. During the first two months, two weekly 1-hour training sessions were completed. During the final two months, one weekly training session was completed, supplemented by one weekly unassisted training session (figure 9). This adds up to 24 assisted and mandatory training sessions and 8 unassisted training sessions. The group-based training sessions involved elements of aerobic exercise (e.g. Nordic Walking, Aerobic), strength training, stretching and games. Furthermore, the participants were introduced to activities in the local area during the 4 months. The physiotherapist or the exercise specialist focused primarily on training to improve aerobic capacity (more than 50% of heart rate reserve for a minimum of 20 minutes) (Sorensen et al., 2007). In a parallel study of EoP in Vejle and Ribe counties, a sub-sample was analysed concerning heart rate during a training session (Sorensen et al., 2007). For the sample of participants, the results indicated that the intensity was on average 76% of maximal heart rate, which is above the minimum training intensity for improving aerobic capacity in a physically inactive population (ACSM, 1998). In general, the training complied with the above-mentioned guidelines for intensity, but more precise descriptions of the training sessions are not possible, since the planning, organisation and execution were entirely controlled by the physiotherapist or exercise specialist and could vary from training session to training session.

In addition, the participants received motivational counselling at baseline and after four months. Subsequently they received voluntary phone based and/or personal motivational counselling after ten and sixteen months. The motivational counselling was based upon the principles of motivational interviewing (Miller & Rollnick, 2002), incorporating the Transtheoretical Model as well (Prochaska & Diclemente, 1983). The aim of the motivational counselling was to increase daily physical activity by influencing central elements described by the Transtheoretical Model (*stages of change, self-efficacy*, decisional balance and processes of change) in cooperation with the participants (Miller & Rollnick, 2002). Furthermore, the counselling concerned the discussion of possible strategies for overcoming barriers towards being physically active. The motivational counselling was carried out by the physiotherapists or exercise specialists. The physiotherapists and exercise specialists had no prior experience conducting motivational interviews, but they were all trained in authorised educational courses selected by the county and municipality. In general, the counselling was used for making a plan of action and a physical activity schedule. The participants were responsible for following the schedule.

In the PG, motivational counselling was the only structured part of the intervention. It was conducted in the same way as in the TG, following the same guidelines. As with the TG, the motivational counselling was provided by physiotherapists or exercise specialists educated along the same guidelines. After initial motivational counselling, the participants in the PG were expected to carry out unassisted training or participate in training in existing local sports clubs (figure 9). The intensity of the unassisted training or activity at local sports clubs is not known, since it varied depending on which activity the participant chose to participate in. Participants in the PG received personal motivational counselling at baseline and after four months. Subsequently they received voluntary phone based and/or personal motivational counselling after ten and sixteen months. Further needs for counselling outside set time schedule were accommodated. The motivational counselling was also based upon the principles of motivational interviewing (Miller & Rollnick, 2002). The aim of the motivational counselling was to increase daily physical activity by influencing central elements described by the Transtheoretical Model (*stages of change, self-efficacy,* decisional balance and processes of change) in cooperation with the participants (Miller & Rollnick, 2002). The participant was responsible for carrying out the schedule.

Even with information from literature of *prescribed exercise* and the EoP initiative in Denmark, there is still a lack of knowledge of how individuals trying to change behaviour during and after *prescribed exercise* are influenced by *stages of change, self-efficacy* and social relations. It is important to recognize the significance of the individual's psychological and social precondition towards behaviour change prior to inclusion into a *prescribed exercise* intervention. It is also important to explore changes in psychological and social conditions during and following the *prescribed exercise* intervention. It is likely that the psychological and social precondition and development is just as important as the intervention itself in terms of gaining long-term effect and persistence in a physically active lifestyle. It is relevant to clarify to what extent differences in *stages of change, self-efficacy* and social relations before, during and after EoP is influencing motivation and adherence towards a physically active lifestyle. An analysis of these factors will be able to contribute with knowledge, which to a higher degree would make it possible for practicians to take into account individual psychosocial circumstances of importance to the individual's physical activity behaviour in future interventions.

38

Aim and Hypotheses

The aim of the current thesis is to increase our understanding of health psychological aspects, of the patient's perspective, in a community-based treatment. The *Exercise on Prescription* intervention is analysed as a case. The effects of treatment intervention (TG) and prevention intervention (PG) on *self-efficacy* concerning barriers, *stages of change,* and physical activity are explored with analyses of levels of *self-efficacy* concerning barriers, levels of *stages of change* and levels of physical activity, to determine if they are influenced to a greater degree in the treatment intervention than in the prevention intervention. Furthermore, the aim is to analyse whether levels of *self-efficacy* concerning barriers and levels of *stages of change* at baseline are different for participants in a treatment intervention compared with participants in a prevention intervention and to determine if such a difference is decisive for long-term levels of physical activity. In addition, another aim is to determine if differences in baseline levels of *self-efficacy* concerning barriers and levels of *stages of change* of participants in both the treatment intervention and prevention intervention are decisive regarding long-term levels of physical activity. Finally, the aim is to analyse to what degree selected social relations influence physical activity behaviour and adherence to a physically active lifestyle.

Hypotheses

1) Participation in the TG and the PG will lead to changes in levels of *self-efficacy* concerning barriers, *stages of change* and physical activity.

2) The initial level of *self-efficacy* toward barriers and *stages of change* will be different for the Treatment Group (TG) and the Prevention Group (PG). Because the PG participants enter the intervention on their own initiative, their psychological precondition is expected to be more positive towards change than the TG. This characteristic could be central to the participants' level of physical activity.

3) The participants' initial level of *self-efficacy* towards barriers and *stages of change* before the intervention is important for adherence to a physically active lifestyle. A positive psychological precondition concerning behaviour change will lead to a higher level of physical activity after intervention.

4) Social relations (e.g., general practitioner (GP), exercise specialist, exercise group, family and friends) are important for the participants' adherence to physical activity during and after EoP.

Methods

Design of the study

The author's role

In general, EoP programmes in Denmark are quite similar to each other in terms of their overarching design and content (e.g., physical activity interventions aiming to treat and reduce the risk of lifestyle diseases) (Sørensen et al., 2010). However, because EoP was initiated without any central coordination, the result is EoP programmes with a variety of differences across counties and municipalities (e.g., length of the physical activity intervention, amount of counselling and duration) (Bredahl et al., 2010). Funen County and Frederiksberg Municipality organised their EoP programmes as described above in "Exercise on Prescription in Funen County and Frederiksberg Municipality". Due to their specific organisation, which deviated from the traditional organisational form of EoP in Denmark, they decided to conduct specific evaluations of their programme.

Centre of Applied and Clinical Exercise Science (ACES), under the direction of Lis Puggaard, Institute of Sports Science and Clinical Biomechanics, University of Southern Denmark, initiated a national evaluation of EoP programmes. The evaluation should gather data from EoP schemes in Denmark. Furthermore, the evaluation should resemble an adjusted Health Technology Assessment (HTA) with a focus on technology (training), patients, organisation and economy (Kristensen & Sigmund, 2007). Generally, a HTA is a multi- and a cross-disciplinary research activity, which provides input for prioritisations and decisions in health services in relation to prevention, diagnostics, treatment and rehabilitation (Kristensen & Sigmund, 2007).

At the beginning of the national evaluation of EoP, a PhD study had already been initiated evaluating technology (training, health benefits and physiological developments of EoP programmes) (Sorensen et al., 2008). Other studies have examined organisational and economic issues (Bredahl et al., 2010; Sørensen et al., 2010). One of the most challenging issues for any EoP is the programme's ability to maintain participants' engagement in a physically active lifestyle during and after completion of the intervention. Moreover, since there is only limited knowledge concerning the extent to which participants who complete an EoP programme continue to be physically active after the supervised training programme has come to an end, Funen and Frederiksberg decided to evaluate the patient perspective of the HTA of EoP.

Because the TG and PG had already been initiated prior to the evaluation of the patient perspective the author had limited possibilities for influencing the research design. The following aspects had already been decided prior to the author's engagement: organisation of the intervention, inclusion criteria, inclusion procedure for the intervention, the training of the participants, the motivational counselling and the continuous contact with the participants. These areas were planned and performed by the intervention manager and health professionals employed in the intervention.

Study intervention

With the given design in mind, the aims, hypotheses and analyses of the thesis emerged through discussions between the author and supervisors. It was clear that due to the already established design, inclusion criteria and procedures of the intervention, it was not possible to conduct a randomised controlled trial.

It became the aim of the current study to conduct an evaluation of best practice (Driever, 2002; Green, 2001) and gain knowledge from Practice Based Evidence (Ramian, 2009). Evaluation can be understood as a comparison of an object or procedure against a standard of acceptability. Evaluation can also be considered as providing an appraisal of what has been done. This could include the suitability or appropriateness of the material used to e.g. collect data. The main purpose of such an evaluation would be to improve the intervention and provide feedback to professionals concerning the strengths and weaknesses of the intervention (Modeste, 1996). Evaluation research generally uses an experimental or quasi-experimental design, conducted to establish the efficacy or effectiveness of an intervention among a defined population (Modeste, 1996). Best practice can be understood as the process of planning and organising the most appropriate intervention for the setting and population rather than as a gold standard or a packaged intervention (Driever, 2002; Green, 2001). Practice Based Evaluation refers to publishable research, with a basis in practice, but without the possibility of incorporating a control group (Hellerstein, 2008; Ramian, 2009). One argument for conducting a practice based evaluation, as opposed to a randomised controlled trial, is that information from a randomised controlled trial, focusing on an isolated practice, to some extent will have limited transfer value for a complex reality. Moreover, although randomised controlled trials are considered to provide the best form of evidence, this does not mean that other research designs are without value. Other studies that provide evidence lower in the hierarchy will also garner important knowledge about relevant associations and inspire other analyses, possibly from randomised controlled trials (Zachariae, 2007). An ideal analysis might combine Evidence Based Practice and Practice Based Evidence (Barkham & Mellor-Clark, 2003). Practice Based Evidence could provide practical and immediately useable answers and possibly raise questions in context, to be answered in further research (Ramian, 2009).

Well aware of not enrolling highest in the evidence hierarchy amongst meta analyses and randomised controlled trials (Edlund et al., 2004; Fox et al., 2007) and aware that potential biases and sources of error could influence data collected, the analyses conducted for this thesis may provide information about the complex reality within which interventions occur (i.e., in counties and municipalities) (Zachariae, 2007). The analyses might also provide valuable information regarding the ongoing development of the EoP scheme.

Due to the way the intervention was designed, the author had no influence on how and which individuals were included in the intervention, no information on different lifestyle diseases, and no influence on how the intervention was carried out. As a logical consequence of this, none of the employed health professionals working with either the TG or the PG could be blinded to which group the participants belonged and what training and counselling they had participated in. Moreover, none of the participants could be blinded to which intervention they were a part of. Furthermore, as a consequence of the predetermined design, the author of the thesis took into account that valuable information from the GPs concerning health status and lifestyle diseases was not available, hence making it impossible to include such information in the analyses. Further, the author of the thesis also took into account that it was not possible to obtain information from the participants before they agreed to participate in either the TG or PG and agreed to be part of the evaluation. Moreover, the author realised that even though it was not possible to let the PG serve as a standard control or reference group, and even though inclusion criteria for the TG and the PG varied, an analysis to determine which intervention form (TG or PG) influenced the participants' psychological condition towards behaviour change more, was relevant. Results from analyses of the hypotheses will be able to qualify and provide practical guidelines for how physical activity interventions in future settings could implement behavioural and health psychological factors, in cooperation with the individual, to better influence and facilitate behaviour change towards a more physically active lifestyle.

Thus, given the basis of the already existing design, the role of the author of the current thesis was the following: in cooperation with supervisors to establish relevant research questions; to establish relevant methods to analyse the aims and hypotheses; to cooperate with health professionals in the county and municipality concerning systematising the gathering of data; to analyse questionnaire data; to conduct, code and analyse interviews; and to write articles and this thesis.

Recruitment and allocation

Recruitment of participants for the TG and the PG in Funen County and Frederiksberg Municipality took place over 21 months, between 2005 and 2007. The EoP intervention was launched 6 months prior to the PhD study. Hence, the TG and the PG were evaluated from November 2005 until May 2008.

All individuals who contacted the physiotherapist and/or the exercise specialist and came to initial meetings in the TG or the PG, and who met the inclusion criteria, were permitted to participate in the study.

The participants and informants (of the qualitative study) were as fully as possible, together with a witness, informed of the overall aim, design, possible risks, and advantages by participating in the study. The participants and informants were informed about the voluntariness of the study and about the possibility to withdraw from the study at any time. The participants and informants brought home written material and were given two days to consider the participation before having to give an answer. Informed consent from all participants and informants in the study was obtained.

Figure 10 provides an overview of the PhD study incorporated in the schematic outline of the Exercise on Prescription intervention in Funen County and Frederiksberg Municipality. Participants included in the study (in both the TG and the PG) were involved in the organised intervention in Funen County and Frederiksberg Municipality. Furthermore, all participants completed questionnaires at specific times during the study (at baseline, 4, 10 and 16 months). A strategically selected target group were interviewed at the same measurement points.

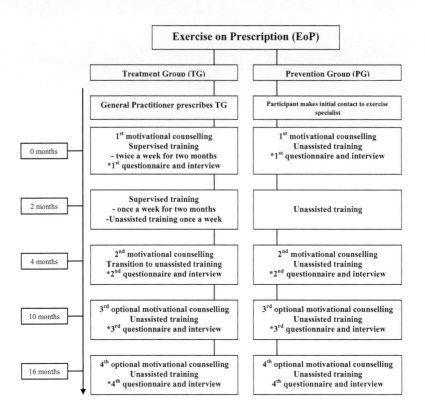

Figure 10. Overview of the PhD study incorporated in to the schematic outline of the Exercise on Prescription intervention in Funen County and Frederiksberg Municipality. Participants in the TG and the PG completed questionnaires and interviews at baseline, 4, 10 and 16 months.

The study was approved by The Danish Data protection Agency (registration number 2005-41-5248). Data were kept secure following the guidelines provided from the agency. The data was stored so nothing was referable to individuals. Names and addresses were changed and files were coded and encrypted. Due to the non-biological and non-treating perspective of the study no registration to the local ethics committee was needed. The study was registered with ClinicalTrials.gov (registration number: NCT00594360).

Outcome measures

The analyses are performed as a triangulation of methods – a combination of quantitative and qualitative methods combined with relevant research literature. The quantitative data are collected through questionnaires and the qualitative data are collected through semi-structured interviews with strategically selected informants (Gubrium & Holstein, 2001).

Information about psychological values and self-reported measures (BMI, physical activity and psychological conditions towards behaviour change) are assessed at baseline and at the time of motivational counselling (figure 10). Interviews are done at the same time points.

Quantitative measures

All self-reported measures were assessed by self-administrated questionnaires distributed by the physiotherapist and/or the exercise specialist at baseline and after four months. After ten and sixteen months the questionnaires were distributed by the author. All questionnaires were returned to the author by mail in pre-paid envelopes.

Translation and validation of the questionnaires

The main part of the overall questionnaire was originally in Danish, but essential parts of the questionnaire were originally in English. All parts with an English origin were translated to Danish by following guidelines:

a) The questionnaires were translated into Danish by a native English speaker. b) Differences in meaning of specific terms and cultural differences between the original and the translated version were discussed by a second party. c) Meaning and cultural differences were adapted to Danish conditions. d) The questionnaire was re-translated into English by a third party. e) Differences in meaning between the original and the retranslated version were discussed and adjusted by a fourth party (Beaton et al., 2000). After translation the questionnaire was tested in a group similar to the participants in the intervention. All irregularities and uncertainties about questions and wording were discussed with the test group and afterwards with a panel of researcher. Corrections to make the questionnaire more applicable to the target group were done (Beaton et al., 2000). Information from the questionnaire was collected in the following three categories:

Socio demographic and basic physiological information

Demographic background variables were assessed by means of the baseline questionnaire. Information about education, personal and household income was gathered along with the person registration number (CPR). Age was calculated from the CPR number. Educational level, personal, and household income was assessed by asking e.g.: "Which kind of school education du you have?" "Do you have completed an education/vocational education?", "Which kind?", "How large was your and your household income last year (before taxes and deductions)?" Bodyweight and height were assessed by asking "Please write your bodyweight in kilos" and "Please write your height in centimetres". BMI was calculated by dividing bodyweight (kg) with height (m) squared.

Psychological factors

Self-efficacy

Self-efficacy in relation to barriers towards physical activity was assessed by a questionnaire (Benisovich et al., 1998; Marcus et al., 1992b). E.g. "I feel convinced that I am able to exercise 3 times or more a week with a duration of at least 20 minutes at a time even though: "I am under a lot of stress", "I feel I don't have the time", "I have to exercise alone", "I don't have access to exercise equipment", "I am spending time with friends or family who do not exercise", and "It's raining or snowing". The final *self-efficacy* score express a summation of the scores of the different *self-efficacy* questions in the questionnaire. The overall score have a range from 18-90.

The participants were dichotomised into high and low level of *self-efficacy*. After analysis of distribution of the participants, the definition of high and low level of *self-efficacy* was determined by separating by median = 57. The participants scoring 57 or less were categorised in to low level of *self-efficacy* whereas participants scoring higher than 57 were categorised into high level of *self-efficacy*. This dichotomisation was done to be able to compare development in physical activity in relation to baseline high or low level of *self-efficacy*.

Stages of change

Studies have used *stages of change* to score individual readiness to change in relation to physical activity (Booth et al., 1993; Hellsten et al., 2008; Marcus et al., 1992b; Marcus et al., 1992a; Marcus & Simkin, 1994; Nigg et al., 1999; Nigg, 2005; Riebe et al., 2005; Sarkin et al., 2001; Schumann et al., 2002; Schumann et al., 2003; Schutzer & Graves, 2004). Most have worked from a cross sectional design and therefore the results from these studies are not directly transferable to this study. *Stages of change* in relation to physical activity was in this study assessed by a questionnaire originally presented by Marcus and colleagues in 1992 (Marcus et al., 1992b) but further developed by Benisovich in 1998 (Benisovich et al., 1998; Nigg et al., 1998; Nigg, 2002; Norman et al., 1998; Reed et al., 1997). Even though the applicability of a smaller 6 item questionnaire, in studies have

46

proven better to detect cross-sectional differences in *stages of change* between groups a continuous measure was selected due to the longitudinal design of this study (Nigg, 2002).

Questions asked in the questionnaire were e.g. "As far as I'm concerned, I don't need to exercise regularly", "I really think I should work on getting started with a regular exercise program in the next 6 months", and "I have started exercising regularly within the last 6 months.

The questionnaire provides a score for six categories of *stages of change* which have been determined of importance in the change process. The six stages are defined as precontemplation non-believers, precontemplation believers, contemplation, preparation, action and maintenance. The questionnaire provides a summarised score for each category (range 4-20). The highest score of the six categories determines which *stage of change* the individual can be categorised to. If scores are equal, the individual are categorised into the lowest of the categories scoring highest (Nigg, 2002). The participants are dichotomised into low and high *stages of change* from following rules: If participants are categorised into precontemplation non-believers, precontemplation believers, contemplation or preparation, they are defined as having a low level of *stages of change*. If participants are categorised into action or maintenance, they are defined as having a high level of *stages of change* (Nigg, 2002). This dichotomisation was done to be able to compare development in physical activity in relation to baseline *stage of change*.

Physical activity

Physical activity is defined as any bodily movement produced by the contraction of skeletal muscles resulting in energy expenditure (Caspersen et al., 1985). Measurement of physical activity should therefore ideally include all physical activity and inactivity 24 hours a day. There is no universally accepted gold standard for measuring all aspects of physical activity (Wareham & Rennie, 1998), although the doubly labelled water method is a valid method for measuring energy expenditure (Conway et al., 2002b). The validity of self-report methods depends on the respondents' ability to accurately assess the different aspects of physical activity. In general, physical activity questionnaires seems to be less sensitive in detecting accurate changes in physical activity than methods of doubly labelled water (Ainslie et al., 2003; Conway et al., 2002a; Staten et al., 2001) accelerometers and pedometers (Conway et al., 2002b). Self-report questionnaires are applicable and easy to administer, and could therefore be the instrument of choice in larger studies. Questionnaires are in general valid for population classification to physical activity levels but are not appropriate for determination of physical activity on an individual level (Rennie & Wareham, 1998). A number of physical activity questionnaires have been validated against other direct or

47

indirect methods for measuring physical activity (Harada et al., 2001; Jacobs et al., 1993; Philippaerts et al., 1999; Philippaerts et al., 2001; Richardson et al., 1994; Staten et al., 2001). Most questionnaires record frequency, duration, and/or intensity of work-related physical activity and/or sports and leisure time activities. Others include specific daily life activities such as climbing stairs, walking, or bicycling. The questionnaires differ in methods used, the way that they are administered, the target population in which they can be used, the time frame over which activity is assessed, the type of activity that is measured, and the scale to which this exposure is reduced. Coefficients of reliability and validity seem to be highest in simple questionnaires assessing physical activity (Shephard, 2003). Moreover, there is a tendency to over-report physical activity and under-report sedentary behaviour (Shephard, 2003). A large number of studies used questionnaires to record the self-reported physical activity (Ainsworth et al., 1993b; Ainsworth et al., 1993a; Booth, 2000; Booth et al., 2002; Conway et al., 2002a; Craig et al., 2003; Dannecker et al., 2003; Jacobs et al., 1993; Paffenbarger et al., 1993; Richardson et al., 1994; Suzuki, 1998; Wareham & Rennie, 1998). Many questionnaires are designed solely to leisure time activities (e.g. sports and exercise), but in this study it is important to be able to record activities throughout the day. It is important that the questionnaire is capable of measuring quantity and type of the physical activity which is in focus in the TG and the PG. Therefore, it is important not only to document changes of physical activity in relation to exercise and sports but any initiated physical activity. Moreover, it is important to be able to detect small or moderate changes in daily physical activity. This could include changes in relation to walking and cycling to and from work (Aadahl & Jorgensen, 2003; Norman et al., 2001). In the TG and the PG the changes which may happen to the individuals are expected to be modest, perhaps even so small that it can be difficult to measure. It is important that the questionnaire used in this study offers the possibility to register longitudinal development, and not just provide a cross-sectional physical activity measure from a target population.

Physical activity in this study was assessed using a questionnaire, allowing daily physical activity to be transformed into energy consumption (MET*hours/day) and conversion to MET (Norman et al., 2001). The questionnaire used for registration of physical activity in this study was originally developed by a Swedish research team (Norman et al., 2001). Reproducibility of the questionnaire done six months apart showed a Spearman correlation coefficient of 0.65. A validation of a questionnaire containing an analogous physical activity questionnaire was done with a similar population by Sorensen and colleagues in 2007 (Sorensen et al., 2007). Agreement percent was for level of physical activity 87-99%.

Statistical analysis

Sample size

To analyse the hypotheses of the study, the questionnaire consist of different scoring instruments used in other studies. Therefore, an overall power calculation of the sample size needed to analyse the full questionnaire was not possible. Instead, power calculations were done for key scoring instruments to indicate the number of participants needed to detect valuable changes. Power calculations were performed to estimate the sample size needed to detect a difference for physical activity. Estimated sample size for two-sample comparison of means done by the "sampsi" command in Stata 9.0 with means of 38 and 40, power as 0.8 and standard deviation as sd1(4) sd2(4) was 63. Estimated sample size for one sample with repeated measures done by the "sampsi" command in Stata 9.0 with the same values was 43 (Kirkwood & Sterne, 2003). Power calculations were also done to estimate the sample size needed to detect a difference for *self-efficacy*. Estimated sample size for one sample with repeated measures done by the "sampsi" command in Stata 9.0 with a mean of 57, alternative mean as 61, power as 0.9 and standard deviation as SD (17) was 190 (Kirkwood & Sterne, 2003). Using these assumptions for the overall study it was decided to try to include a sample size of 190 in each group. 213 and 124 was included to the TG and the PG at baseline, respectively.

Statistics

In the quantitative study, the primary objectives were to analyse changes in levels of *self-efficacy*, *stages of change* and physical activity within and between the TG and the PG, to analyse baseline values of *self-efficacy* and *stages of change* and relate these to level and development of physical activity. Furthermore, a goal was to determine if differences in baseline *self-efficacy* and *stages of change* between participants in the TG and the PG effect levels of physical activity. Thus, linear growth curve analyses (LGC) – a special case of multilevel linear regression were used (Rabe-Hesketh & Skrondal, 2008). The advantage of LGC analysis is that it allows the estimation of individual change as a function of time. The LGC analysis hypothesises that, for each individual, the continuous outcome variable is a simple linear function of time, called the individual growth trajectory, plus error. The resemblance between LGC and regular multiple linear regression is close, though with at least two important differences. In addition to the parameters of initial levels (intercept) and rate of increase/decrease (slope) of the outcome of interest, LGC divides the variance of these parameters into estimates of individual intercept variability, slope variability and intra-individual residual variability. Using standard notation (Rabe-Hesketh & Skrondal, 2008), the variability terms are named intercept-variance (ψ_i), slope variance (ψ_s) and residual variance (θ), respectively. The intercept and slope variance represent random deviation from the population mean of both parameters (inter-individual variability). Residual variance represents a summary of individual random deviation between the estimated individual trajectory and the true individual (intra-individual variance) (Singer & Willet, 2003). The estimated individual intercepts and slopes are assumed to be random; hence a random term for these parameters is included when specifying the model. Another important difference between regular multiple linear regression and LGC is that LGC takes into account that the observed individual values at adjacent points in time are correlated, thereby providing more accurate estimates of the standard errors. For analyses including *stages of change* as the outcome measure, random-effect logistic regression was used, though restricted to models that included a random intercept only. All analyses were performed using STATA version 10.0. A p-value less than 0.05 were considered statistically significant.

The outcome variables, including level of physical activity, level of *self-efficacy* and level of *stages of change*, were plotted against time as a linear and non-linear transformation and inspected visually. In the present analyses, the measurement of time as a simple linear measurement with measurement points equally spaced was used. Thus, time was coded 0 for 'baseline', 1 for '4 months', 2 for '10 months' and 3 for '16 months', and time was entered as a categorical variable in all LGC models.

A taxonomy of three growth curve models was fitted to facilitate systematic evaluation of the fixed effects and the variance components (Singer & Willet, 2003). In model 1, the overall rate of change of the outcome of interest (physical activity, *self-efficacy* and *stages of change*) was estimated by fitting a model that included time and a random term for the intercept and slope. Model 1 allowed an estimation of the degree of individual variance in initial level and growth in level of *self-efficacy* or physical activity. In model 2, the measure that classified participants as members of the TG or the PG was added. In model 3, an interaction term of group-by-time was included to facilitate estimation of a possible difference in rate of change in, e.g., levels of *self-efficacy* (or physical activity) for participants classified as members of the TG versus the PG. A logistic individual growth curve model was fitted for the analysis of individual *stages of change* (i.e., as a dichotomous outcome).

Baseline analysis

Comparisons of socio-demographic and basic physiological factors between the TG and the PG at baseline were assessed by independent t-tests and Chi-Square tests (Altman, 1999).

Following the analyses of the hypotheses by LGC analyses, baseline differences in socio-demographic factors between the TG and the PG were introduced into the LGC analyses as covariates for each time point. Results from the baseline analyses are presented as model 4 in tables in the results section. Results from these analyses and possible differences from output in model 3 due to the influence of covariates are addressed in the results and discussion section of the thesis.

Fluctuation in number of participants in the analyses

The number of participants included in the different analyses varies depending on which variable is being analysed. If participants did not sufficiently complete items (e.g., they did not complete information regarding physical activity) for a specific time point, their data are omitted from the analysis for that time point, but included again at the next time point if sufficient information was collected. As a consequence of this, data from an individual participant might be included in analyses of, e.g., physical activity but not for *self-efficacy* at a given time point. In analyses including both *self-efficacy* and physical activity, for example, data for a participant are omitted from analyses if data for just one of the two variables are missing.

Drop-out analysis

Following LGC analyses of the hypotheses, drop-out analyses were performed to clarify whether drop-outs differed from those individuals who participated. In the drop-out analyses, missing values were coded (1) and observed values were coded (0). Afterwards, the likelihood of having missing values for each outcome variable was compared to the likelihood of having an observed value. This was done through logistic regression analysis including independent socio-demographic variables (gender, age, income, BMI and education) at each time-point (Verbeke & Molenberghs, 2000). If one of these independent variables statistically significantly predicted having missing values, the effect of the variable on outcome variables was analysed as well. To analyse the effect of drop-outs on outcome variables, missing data due to drop-outs or insufficient completion of questionnaires were imputed by "last observation carried forward" (McKnight et al., 2007; Shao & Zhong, 2003; Verbeke & Molenberghs, 2000). If a value for a specific outcome variable was not obtainable at baseline, the value from the subsequent time point was carried backwards. Outcome (*self-efficacy*, *stages of change* and physical activity) values from participants were compared to outcome values from both participants and drop-outs in long-term (16 months). This was done to determine if

51

inclusion of drop-outs in the analyses statistically significantly influenced the findings, thus indicating biased results due to drop-outs. The analyses were done with data from 16 months because drop-out rates were expected to be the greatest at that time point. The consequences of drop-outs are discussed in relation to the specific analyses performed and presented in the results section of the thesis.

Qualitative measures

The aim of the qualitative study was to substantiate, elaborate and supplement the quantitative data and, furthermore, to address hypothesis four (Fox et al., 2007). The hypotheses were explored with semi-structured in-depth interviews, to explore and evaluate the participants' *self-efficacy* in relation to barriers, initial level of and development in *stages of change,* and furthermore, the impact of social relations on levels of physical activity. The materials gathered from the interviews were to investigate the hypotheses. The design of the semi-structured in-depth interviews was modified to allow for the opportunity to pursue new and relevant issues raised by answers to the interview questions (Dahler-Larsen, 2005; Olsen, 2002).

Interview guide
The interview guide was divided into specific themes and consisted of several main categories concerning background as well as social and psychological issues. Under each theme, specific working questions were formulated (figure 11) (Kvale, 2003).

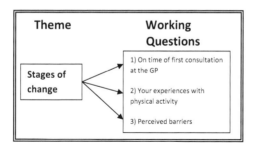

Figure 11. From theme to working questions in the qualitative design

Each informant was interviewed at baseline and after 4, 10 and 16 months. All interviews were performed in the informants' homes by the author and were digitally recorded. The average duration of the interviews was 45 to 60 minutes (Olsen, 2002) (Appendix B: Baseline interview guide).

Sample size
The informants were chosen from amongst the participants in the TG and the PG. Inclusion criteria were applied to assure that information gathered would provide in-depth knowledge from the participants in the two projects. Different factors made the selection of informants challenging such as the skewed distribution of gender (a large percentage of the participants were women (63 percent

53

in TG and 78 percent in PG)) and age (the age of the participants in the interventions varied from 21 to 83 years of age, with a mean age of 54 years). Income, education and work status varied as well. The general conclusion from these factors was that it was difficult to select representative informants in relation to participants in the two interventions (TG and PG). Informants could therefore be selected from different criteria dependent on the output wanted (Kvale, 2003; Olsen, 2002). Selection criteria could e.g. be "mean" or "marginal" informants, women because of their high percentage in the intervention or informants from different groups to gain knowledge from all areas (Denzin & Lincoln, 2005).

Based upon the above mentioned considerations, strategically selected key informants from different groups were asked to participate in the interview study (Kvale, 2003). Selection criteria included age, gender, TG or PG, income, educational background and employment, and these were used to assure that information gathered was adequate to represent a broad range of participants in the two projects. Only those individuals who signed a written consent were included in the study. Because of the intensive information to be gathered from the participants in this qualitative study, the sample was limited to four informants from each intervention (table 3). One informant from PG did not attend the first interview and were therefore excluded from the study. Hence, only 3 informants from the PG were a part of the study. In TG, two participants were from Funen County and two were from Frederiksberg Municipality. One man and three women at the age span of 48-59 were chosen. The informants had different income and educational background. Their work status varied from unemployed to working (table 3). In PG, one participant was from Funen County and two were from Frederiksberg Municipality. One man and two women at the age span of 52-82 were chosen. The informants had different income and educational background. Their work status varied from sick leave to pension (table 3).

TG	Age±SD	Women (%)	Education 1*	Education 2**	Income, Own (in thousands) ***	Income, Household (in thousands) ***	Work status	County
Overall	56±12 (Range 22-82)	63	4.0±1.1 (10-11 years of school)	4.6±1.6	5.5±3.4	7.9±3.4	----	----
1	55	M	8-9 years of school	Education as semi-skilled worker	150- 199	150- 199	Sick leave	Funen
2	51	K	Highschool level	Medium length higher education	350 - 399	350 - 399	Working	Funen
3	59	K	10-11 years of school	Shorter higher education	250 - 299	250 - 299	Sick leave	Frederiksberg
4	48	K	10-11 years of school	Other technical education	100 - 149	100 - 149	Un employed	Frederiksberg
PG	Age±SD	Women (%)	Education 1*	Education 2**	Income, Own (in thousands) ***	Income, Household (in thousands)***	Work status	County
Overall	51±14 (Range 21-83)	78	3.9±1.1	4.8±1.5	4.6±3.3	6.9±3.6	----	----
5	82	K	8-9 years of school	Other technical education	250 - 299	250 - 299	Pension	Frederiksberg
6	68	M	8-9 years of school	Shorter higher education	250 - 299	350 - 399	Pension	Frederiksberg
7	52	K	10-11 years of school	Shorter higher education	250 - 299	Over 700	Disability pension	Funen

Table 3. Distribution of gender, age, education, income, work status, and county for the informants of the TG and the PG
*Education 1: 1= Goes to school, 2= 7 or fewer years of school, 3= 8-9 years of school, 4= 10-11 years of school, 5= High school level, 6= Other (Statens Institut for Folkesundhed, 2006).
**Education 2: 1= Education as semi-skilled worker, 2= basic education of business school, 3= apprentice education or similar, 4= Other technical education, 5= Shorter higher education, 6= medium length higher education, 7= Long higher education (Statens Institut for Folkesundhed, 2006).
***Income in Danish Crowns: 1= 0 – 99,000; 2= 100,000 - 149,000; 3= 150,000 - 199,000; 4= 200,000 - 249,000; 5= 250,000 - 299,000; 6= 300,000 - 349,000; 7= 350,000 - 399,000; 8= 400,000 - 499,000; 9= 500,000 - 599,000; 10= 600,000 - 699,000; 11= Over 700,000 (Statens Institut for Folkesundhed, 2006).

Control of analysis

For the reader to be able to evaluate the author's interpretations of the interviews as much as possible of the context, the authors' perspective, objective, and work procedure is presented. This is done to obtain transparency and to justify interpretations (Kvale, 2003).

Transcribing, condensation and coding

Thematic analysis began when the data were compiled using the semi-structured interview guide. Interviews were transcribed verbatim based on predetermined rules of transcription decided by the author and the transcriber. The rules are described in box 2.

---

a) The interviews are transcribed verbatim.

b) No interpretation of meaning must be done by the transcriber. It is important that the informants own statements are put forward.

c) The transcriptions are divided so that it is obvious who is talking. The researcher and the informant are initially marked by their (or their synonym) initials.

d) When the dialogue change from informant to researcher line is changed.

e) Breaks and pauses for thought are marked by …

f) Linguistic contamination as "er" or other words with no meaning to the context are left out of the transcription.

Box 2. Rules of transcription (Gubrium & Holstein, 2001)

Coding was primarily deductive and based upon the theoretical framework, the hypotheses and the pre-established themes of the interview guides (Olsen, 2002). The data were sorted under different headings in order to identify unique psychological features relevant for adherence with physical activity. To make the coding more precise and increase inter-rater reliability, agreements on coding categories and interpretation were reached by having the author and a colleague analyse the same interview followed by a discussion and adjustment of differences (Olsen, 2002). All of the subsequent coding was done by the author. After coding and reading the interviews through as a whole, the author condensed the interviews by removing recurrences and digressions. Pauses and unclear linguistic expressions were removed from the text. The author carried out a meaning condensation; i.e., the informants' expressed statements were written together to form shorter phrasing and more concise sentences (Kvale, 2003).

Benefits, risk and confidentially

The benefits should exceed the risks of participating in the study. In this study the interviews gave the informant the opportunity to discuss in-depth issues already mentioned in their conversations with the exercise specialist. By confronting the informant with conflicting statements in the interviews, a risk of breaking down their initial confidence existed. Ideally, effort from the participant and the gain from the study should be balanced. A positive effect from the interviews was expected and therefore the yield was considered to be higher that the risks (Kvale, 2003).

Data concerning private issues referable to the individual e.g. names and specific statements were changed. Files were coded and encrypted.

Results

In the following section, the results from the two studies will be presented separately, starting with the quantitative results. Both the quantitative and the qualitative studies analyse hypotheses one, two and three, but hypothesis four is solely analysed qualitatively. The results will be presented in the following order: *self-efficacy*, *stages of change* and physical activity.

Quantitative results

In the following sections, the baseline characteristics will be presented first. Then, results will be presented in relation to the specific hypotheses. Results from hypotheses one and two will be presented jointly due to their connectedness. Results will be presented in the following order: *self-efficacy*, then *stages of change* and lastly results from physical activity.

Baseline characteristics

Statistically significant differences could be seen between the groups in age (56±12 vs. 51±14, p=0.002), gender (63% and 78 % female, respectively) (DF=1, p=0.005), own income (5.5±3.4 vs. 4.6±3.3 p=0.014) and household income (7.9±3.4 vs. 6.9±3.6, p=0.031). No significant baseline differences could be found between the two groups in education and BMI (table 4).

	TG	PG	p-value	N	All
Age	56±12	51±14	0.00	213/124	54±13
Female %	63%	78%	DF=1 0.005	--------	68 %
Education (1)*	4.0±1.1	3.9±1.1	0.68	208/121	3.9±1.1
Education (2)**	4.6±1.6	4.8±1.5	0.53	152/91	4.7±1.5
Income (Own)***	5.5±3.4	4.6±3.3	0.01	189/118	5.2±3.4
Income (household)***	7.9±3.4	6.9±3.6	0.03	156/101	7.5±3.5
BMI	31.9±5.7	31.7±6.7	0.37	211/120	31.8±6.0

Table 4. Baseline comparison between the TG and the PG and standard deviation (SD) in age, gender, education, income and BMI.
*Education 1: 1= Goes to school, 2= 7 or fewer years of school, 3= 8-9 years of school, 4= 10-11 years of school, 5= High school level, 6= Other (Statens Institut for Folkesundhed, 2006). **Education 2: 1= Education as semi-skilled worker, 2= basic education of business school, 3= apprentice education or similar, 4= Other technical education, 5= Shorter higher education, 6= medium length higher education, 7= Long higher education (Statens Institut for Folkesundhed, 2006). ***Income in Danish Crowns: 1= 0 – 99,000; 2= 100,000 – 149,000; 3= 150,000 – 199,000; 4= 200,000 – 249,000; 5= 250,000 – 299,000; 6= 300,000 – 349,000; 7= 350,000 – 399,000; 8= 400,000 – 499,000; 9= 500,000 – 599,000; 10= 600,000 – 699,000; 11= Over 700,000 (Statens Institut for Folkesundhed, 2006).

Drop-outs

Drop-outs were registered when they did not turn in their questionnaires. If participants did not submit a questionnaire for a given time point, they were excluded from the study and not given the opportunity to answer subsequent questionnaires. As seen in figure 12 the overall drop-out rate in both intervention groups were quite high. In the TG a 27 %, 16% and 10% drop-out at 4, 10 and 16 months were current. In the PG a 27%, 21% and 11% drop-out at 4, 10 and 16 months were current. This illustrates an overall drop-out rate of 45% in TG and 48 % in PG (figure 12). Details of the sample and number of observations at different points in time are provided in table 5. Table 5 illustrates the fluctuation of the number of participants by the different sample sizes included in analyses of *self-efficacy*, *stages of change* and physical activity at the given time points (table 5).

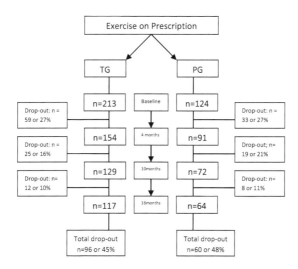

Figure 12. Drop-out from the TG and the PG during the intervention.

Variables	n	Percent
Baseline		
TG	213	63.2
PG	124	36.8
Level of physical activity	267	100
Self-efficacy	314	100
High level of stages of change	302	31.1
4 months		
TG	154	62.9
PG	91	37.1
Level of physical activity	179	67.0^a
Self-efficacy	228	72.6^b
High level of stages of change	223	56.9
10 months		
TG	129	64.2
PG	72	35.8
Level of physical activity	160	59.9
Self-efficacy	183	56.9
High level of stages of change	181	56.9
16 months		
TG	117	64.6
PG	64	35.3
Level of physical activity	122	45.7
Self-efficacy	162	51.6
High level of stages of change	159	45.3

Table 5. Number of observations and attrition from baseline to 16 month
a) Percentage relative to number of observations of level of physical activity at baseline
b) Percentage relative to number of observations of *self-efficacy* at baseline

Self-efficacy (hypothesis one and two)

In the analyses including *self-efficacy* as the outcome measure, model 1 revealed a mean level of *self-efficacy* at baseline of 56.12 (SE = 0.99, p = 0.00), but no statistically significantly change in level of *self-efficacy* across the subsequent measurement points in time was observed (table 6). The initial level of *self-efficacy* varied considerably between participants across the measured points in time (ψ_i = 152.07, SE = 23.84, p = 0.00), as did the individual rate of change (ψ_s = 10.28, SE = 5.19, p = 0.00). Although, the study failed to observe a change in level of *self-efficacy* across the measurement points in time, the measure identifying the two groups of participants in model 2 was introduced to investigate possible differences. Results of the estimates for the grouping variable were observed to be statistically significant (β = 4.13, SE = 1.79, p = 0.02), suggesting that the initial level of *self-efficacy* at baseline was higher for the TG compared to the PG. The variance components remained essentially unchanged, though the residual variance fell from 169 to 159, which amounts to a reduction of 5.76%. Still, the residual variance was observed to be statistically significant (θ = 158.99, SE = 11.59, p = 0.00). In model 3, possible differences concerning changes in level of *self-efficacy* for the two groups at each measurement point in time were investigated. No statistically significant differences were observed between the groups at any point in time. Regarding the variance components, the intercept variance decreased 2.3%, compared to the estimate observed in model 1. The marginal change in the variance component estimates suggests that the grouping variable does not serve as an important predictor of initial level of *self-efficacy* or as a predictor of change in level of *self-efficacy* over time (table 6). Figure 13 illustrates development in level of *self-efficacy* across all time points for the TG and the PG (figure 13).

To determine if the above results were affected by baseline differences between members of the TG and the PG, gender, age and income were introduced into the LGC analyses as covariates. The results indicate that income is a statistically significant covariate in relation to levels of *self-efficacy*. Although, the introduction of covariates in the analyses alters the values of levels of *self-efficacy*, there were no statistically significant differences between model 3 and model 4. At 10 months, the difference between the TG and the PG tends to be significant, which indicates that income as a covariate to some extent influences outcome in terms of levels of *self-efficacy* at 10 months. Including a greater number of participants in the analyses could potentially have demonstrated a statistically significant difference at this time point (table 6, model 4). But since no other values were affected by covariates, it could be concluded that findings from model 3 (table 6) are generally not affected by baseline differences between the TG and the PG. Figure 14 illustrates development in levels of *self-efficacy* across all time points for the TG and the PG after introducing covariates (figure 14).

Drop-out analyses in relation to levels of *self-efficacy* indicated a statistically significant difference between participants and drop-outs in terms of gender at 10 months. Thus, the male gender predicted missing values for *self-efficacy* at 10 months. Table 7 illustrates drop-out analyses of gender, age, income and education in relation to *self-efficacy* at 10 months (table 7). No other differences between participants and drop-outs were shown across all time points. To analyse the effect of drop-outs on *self-efficacy*, imputed data from missing values were introduced into the comparison of *self-efficacy* between the TG and the PG at 16 months. With the introduction of drop-out values, minor changes in levels of *self-efficacy* occurred (TG without missing = 55.73 [52.0-59.4] and TG including missing = 55.38 [51.9-58.9]; PG without missing = 51.63 [46.7-56.5] and PG including missing = 51.51 [46.8-56.2], but there were no statistically significant differences between the groups after inclusion of drop-outs in the analysis, thus indicating that drop-outs do not influence the analysed values of levels of *self-efficacy*.

Variables	Model 1 β (SE)	p-value	Model 2 β (SE)	p-value	Model 3 β (SE)	p-value	Model 4 β (SE)	p-value
Fixed part								
Baseline	56.12 (0.99)	0.00	53.50 (1.50)	0.00	54.19 (1.62)	0.00	57.66 (5.38)	0.00
4 months	-0.17 (1.17)	0.89	-0.18 (1.17)	0.88	-1.56 (1.91)	0.42	-1.93 (2.25)	0.39
10 months	-1.53 (1.33)	0.25	-1.54 (1.33)	0.25	-3.74 (2.17)	0.09	-5.11 (2.56)	0.04
16 months	-1.87 (1.49)	0.21	-1.88 (1.49)	0.21	-2.56 (2.44)	0.29	-3.94 (2.89)	0.17
TG at baseline			4.13 (1.79)	0.02	3.02 (2.03)	0.14	1.62 (2.37)	0.49
TG at 4 months					2.21 (2.42)	0.36	3.67 (2.88)	0.20
TG at 10 months					3.53 (2.75)	0.20	6.14 (3.30)	0.06
TG at 16 months					1.08 (3.08)	0.73	2.99 (3.68)	0.41
Female							-2.68 (2.10)	0.20
Age at baseline							-0.76 (0.82)	0.35
Income (percentiles)							0.76 (0.33)	0.02
Random part								
Intercept variance[a] ψ_i	152.07 (23.84)	0.00	148.54 (23.67)	0.00	148.61 (23.62)	0.00	116.35 (25.68)	0.00
Slope variance[b] ψ_s	10.28 (5.19)	0.04	10.33 (5.20)	0.04	10.40 (5.19)	0.05	10.19 (6.12)	0.10
Residual variance[c] θ	168.71 (11.57)	0.00	158.99 (11.59)	0.00	158.36 (11.56)	0.00	155.09 (13.82)	0.00

Table 6. Estimates and standard error (SE) of changes in levels of *self-efficacy* among the TG and the PG. Total sample sizes of all (both the TG and the PG) participants for the given time points (displayed in chronological sequence) were: baseline, n = 314; 4 months, n = 228; 10 months, n = 183; and 16 months, n =162.

    a) Intercept variance represents random deviation from the population mean in initial level of *self-efficacy*

    b) Slope variance represents random deviation from the population mean of change in *self-efficacy*

    c) Residual variance represents a summary of individual random deviation between the estimated individual trajectory and the true individual score

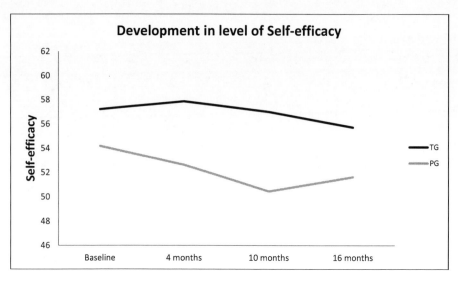

Figure 13. Development in level of *self-efficacy* across time points for the TG and the PG. Number of participants for the given time points (displayed in chronological sequence) were: TG: n = 197, n = 144, n = 115 and n = 102; PG: n = 117, n = 84, n = 68 and n = 60.

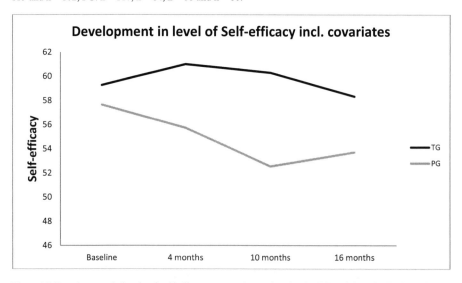

Figure 14. Development in levels of *self-efficacy* across time points for the TG and the PG after introducing covariates (model 4). Number of participants for the given time points (displayed in chronological sequence) were: TG: n = 125, n = 94, n = 71 and n = 68; and PG: n = 85, n = 58, n = 47 and n = 41.

Self-efficacy Variables	Odds Ratio	Std. error	Z	p-value	95% Conf. Interval	
Female	0.156	0.137	-2.12	0.03	0.028	0.872
Age	1.046	0.045	1.04	0.29	0.961	1.138
Income	1.257	0.210	1.37	0.17	0.906	1.745
BMI	0.877	0.067	-1.71	0.09	0.755	1.019
Education (1)	1.288	0.568	0.57	0.57	0.543	3.059
Education (2)	0.926	0.309	-0.23	0.82	0.481	1.783
Number (n) =	105					
LR chi2(6) =	14.57					
Prob > chi2 =	0.024					
Log likelihood =	-25.736					
Pseudo R2 =	0.221					

Table 7. Logistic regression analysis of missing values at 10 months for levels of *self-efficacy*. The table shows a statistically significantly higher probability for having missing values in relation to levels of *self-efficacy* for males.

Stages of change (hypothesis one and two)

In this section results from analyses of hypothesis one and two are presented.

A series of multilevel logistic regression models were conducted in analyses with high level of *stages of change* as the outcome measure. In model 1, the odds ratio of high level of *stages of change* was statistically significantly higher across all measurement points in time, compared to baseline (table 8). The individual level of *stages of change* varied between participants across the measurement points in time (ψ_i = 1.17, 95% CI = 0.90 – 1.49), as did the dependency of the responses for the same individual (θ = 0.31, 95% CI = - 0.18 – 0.80). Thus, the statistically significant estimate of intra-individual variance suggests that measures of *stages of change* across time are rather unstable and that other time-varying factors may explain this variability. In model 2, the grouping variable was added to the equation. A statistically significant higher probability of reporting high levels of *stages of change* at baseline was observed among members of the TG, compared to members of the PG (OR = 1.78, 95%; CI = 1.81 – 2.68). Differences in the probability of reporting high levels of *stages of change* between the two groups of participants across all measurements point in time were investigated in model 3. A statistically significant baseline difference between the TG and the PG could be found. Hence, there was a higher probability of reporting high *stages of change* at baseline for members of the TG. However, no statistically significant differences were observed at other time points. Estimates of the variance components remained essentially unchanged (table 8). Figure 15 illustrates the development in odds-ratio of high level of *stages of change* across time points for the TG and the PG.

To determine if the above results were affected by baseline differences between the TG and the PG, gender, age and income were introduced into the LGC analyses as covariates. Results indicate that age at baseline is a statistically significant covariate in relation to *stages of change*. The introduction of covariates into the analyses alters values of levels of *stages of change* to some extent and leads to the disappearance of the baseline differences between the TG and the PG. No other statistically significant differences between model 3 and model 4 were apparent (table 8, model 4). Since no other values were affected by the covariates, it can be concluded that the results in model 3 (table 8) in general are not affected by baseline differences between the TG and the PG. Figure 16 illustrates the development in levels of *stages of change* across all time points for the TG and the PG after introducing covariates (figure 16).

Drop-out analyses in relation to *stages of change* indicated statistically significant differences between participants and drop-outs at 4 months. Thus, lower education (1) predicts drop-outs or missing values for *stages of change* at 4 months (figure 17). Table 9 illustrates drop-out analyses of gender, age, income and education in relation to *stages of change* at 4 months (table 9). No other differences between participants and drop-outs were shown across all time points. To analyse the effect of drop-outs on *stages of change*, imputed data from missing values were introduced into the comparison of *stages of change* between the TG and the PG at 16 months. With the introduction of drop-out values, minor changes in *stages of change* occurred (TG without missing = 4.08 [3.7-4.4] and TG including missing = 4.07 [3.8-4.4]; PG without missing = 3.75 [3.3-4.2] and PG including missing = 3.79 [3.4-4.2]. No statistically significant differences between the groups after inclusion of drop-outs in the analyses were found, indicating that drop-outs did not influence the analysed values of levels of *stages of change*.

Variables	Model 1 OR (95% CI)	p-value	Model 2 OR (95% CI)	p-value	Model 3 OR (95% CI)	p-value	Model 4 OR (95% CI)	p-value
Fixed part								
Baseline	ref	-	ref	-	ref	-	ref	-
4 months	3.13 (2.10-4.65)	0.00	3.14 (2.11-4.66)	0.00	3.61 (1.89-6.91)	0.00	3.01 (1.42-6.37)	0.00
10 months	3.18 (2.08-4.86)	0.00	3.18 (2.08-4.86)	0.00	2.90 (1.45-5.79)	0.00	2.52 (1.13-2.52)	0.02
16 months	1.97 (1.29-3.02)	0.00	1.97 (1.28-3.01)	0.00	1.91 (0.93-3.93)	0.07	2.43 (1.06-5.5)	0.03
TG at baseline			1.78 (1.81-2.68)	0.01	1.82 (1.01-3.26)	0.04	1.48 (0.74-2.92)	0.27
TG at 4 months					0.79 (0.35-1.77)	0.58	0.87 (0.33-2.24)	0.77
TG at 10 months					1.16 (0.49-2.75)	0.73	1.40 (0.50-3.91)	0.51
TG at 16 months					1.04 (0.43-2.53)	0.93	0.59 (0.20-1.67)	0.32
Female							1.02 (0.63-1.65)	0.91
Age at baseline							1.03 (1.00-1.04)	0.01
Income (percentiles)							1.04 (0.96-.11)	0.31
Random part								
Intercept variance[a] ψ_i	1.17 (0. 90-1.49)	0.00	1.13 (0.87-1.46)	0.00	1.14 (0.88-1.47)	0.00	0.93 (0.63-1.35)	0.00
Residual variance[b] θ	0.31 (-0.18-0.80)	0.39	0.25 (-0.26-0.76)	0.32	0.25 (-0.26-0.77)	0.32	-0.14 (-0.89-0.60)	1.00

Table 8. Odds ratio (OR) and 95% confidence interval of change in odds-ratio of *stages of change* among TG and PG participants. The number of all (both the TG and the PG) participants for the given time points (displayed in chronological sequence) were: n = 302, n = 223, n = 181 and n = 159.
a) Intercept variance represents random deviation from the population mean if initial level of *stages of change*
b) Residual variance represents a summary of individual random deviation between the estimated individual trajectory and the true individual score

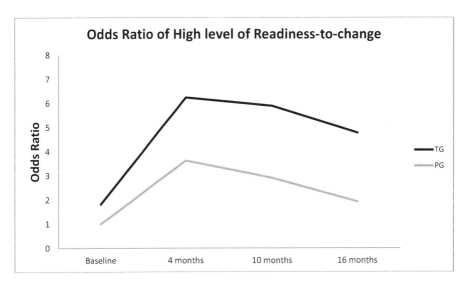

Figure 15. Development in odds-ratio of high level of *stages of change* across time points for TG and PG. The number of participants for the given time points (displayed in chronological sequence) were: TG: n =188, n = 139, n = 113 and n = 101; and PG: n = 114, n = 84, n = 68 and n = 58.

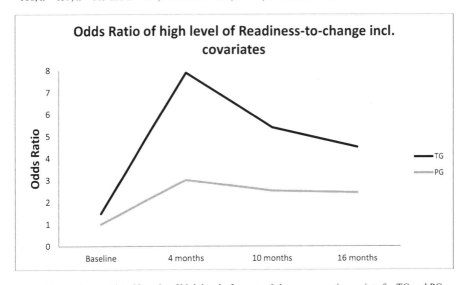

Figure 16. Development in odds-ratio of high level of *stages of change* across time points for TG and PG after introducing covariates (model 4). Number of participants for the given time points (displayed in chronological sequence) were: TG: n = 131, n = 98, n = 81 and n = 75; and PG: n = 86, n = 64, n = 51 and n = 45.

Stages of Change Variables	Odds Ratio	Std. error	Z	p-value	95% Conf. Interval	
Female	0.336	0.346	-1.06	0.29	0.044	2.523
Age	0.994	0.040	-0.14	0.89	0.918	1.077
Income	0.703	0.127	-1.95	0.051	0.494	1.001
BMI	0.992	0.087	-0.09	0.93	0.835	1.179
Education (1)	0.252	0.174	-2.00	0.04	0.065	0.976
Education (2)	1.754	0.861	1.14	0.25	0.670	4.593
Number (n) =	123					
LR chi2(6) =	11.02					
Prob > chi2 =	0.088					
Log likelihood =	-18.47					
Pseudo R2 =	0.229					

Table 9. Logistic regression analysis of missing values at 4 months for levels of *stages of change*. The table shows a statistically significant higher probability for having missing values in relation to *stages of change* with lower education (1).

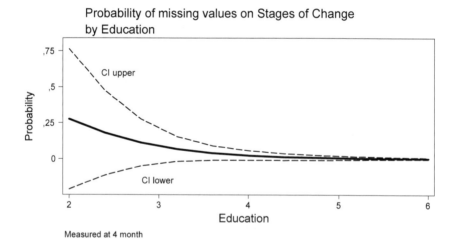

Probability of missing values on Stages of Change by Education

Measured at 4 month

Figure 17. The figure illustrates that the probability of drop-outs or missing values for levels of *stages of change* at 4 months increases with decreasing education (1).

Physical activity (hypothesis one and two)

In this section results from analyses of hypothesis one and two are presented.

In the first LGC analysis, the overall mean level of physical activity was calculated as a function of time (model 1). The model yielded a mean level of physical activity at baseline of 38.70 MET (SE = 0.28, p = 0.00), and a steady increase across the subsequent measurement points in time (table 10). The initial level of physical activity varied considerably between participants across the measured points in time (ψ_i = 16.05, SE = 1.86, p = 0.00). The individual rate of change varied modestly (ψ_s = 0.46, SE = 0.24, p = 0.06). The residual variance was also observed to be statistically significant (θ = 5.87, SE = 0.51, p = 0.00). The observed variability in rate of change showed a trend towards significance but was statistical non-significant. However, because the grouping variable was the focal predictor, it was decided to include the term in subsequent models to explore the full spectrum of its effect. Model 2 included the same predictors as model 1, as well as the measure identifying the two groups of participants. Results of model 2 were essentially the same as model 1, with estimates of the grouping variable being non-significant (β = 0.43, SE = 0.52, p = 0.41), suggesting that the initial level of physical activity at baseline was not different for the two groups of participants. More interesting was that the estimates of the intercept and slope variance, respectively, also remained unchanged. This suggests that the initial level of physical activity and change in physical activity were not affected by classification of the participants into the TG or PG groups. In model 3, possible differences in changes in level of physical activity for the two groups, specifically for each measurement point in time were investigated. Results from the final model suggested no statistically significant differences in changes in level of physical activity between the groups at any point in time. Moreover, the statistically significant increase in mean level of physical activity from baseline to 16 months observed in the preceding models was not significant at 4, 10 and 16 months. The intercept and slope variance remained essentially unchanged, as indicated in previous models (table 10). Figure 18 illustrates development in level of physical activity across all time point for the TG and the PG (figure 18).

To determine if the above results were affected by baseline differences between the TG and PG, gender, age and income were introduced into the LGC analyses as covariates. Results indicated that none of the covariates could be shown as statistically significant in relation to levels of physical activity. Although, the introduction of covariates into the analyses alters values of levels of physical activity, no statistically significant differences between model 3 and model 4 were seen in comparisons between the TG and the PG. With the introduction of the covariates, the results suggest a tendency to a statistically significant increase in overall levels of physical activity from baseline to 16 months. Since none of the covariates were statistically significant, it can be concluded that the results from model 3 (table 10) in general are not affected by baseline differences between the TG and the PG (table 10, model 4). Figure 19 illustrates development in levels of physical activity across all time points for the TG and the PG after introducing covariates (figure 19).

Drop-out analyses in relation to physical activity indicated statistically significant differences between participants and drop-outs at 10 months; higher BMI scores and lower education (2) predict drop-outs or missing values for physical activity at 10 months (figures 20 and 21). Table 11 presents drop-out analyses of gender, age, income and education in relation to physical activity at 10 months (table 11). No differences between participants and drop-outs were found at 4 and 16 months. To analyse the effect of drop-outs on physical activity, imputed data from missing values were introduced into the comparison of physical activity between the TG and the PG at 16 months. With the introduction of drop-out values, minor changes in physical activity occurred (TG without missing = 40.96 [39.8-42.1] and TG including missing = 40.53 [39.6-41.5]; PG without missing = 39.46 [37.8-41.1] and PG including missing = 39.82 [38.5-41.1]. There were no statistically significant differences between the groups after inclusion of drop-outs in the analyses, indicating that drop-outs did not influence analysed values of physical activity.

Variables	Model 1 β (SE)	p-value	Model 2 β (SE)	p-value	Model 3 β (SE)	p-value	Model 4 β (SE)	p-value
Fixed part								
Baseline	38.70 (0.28)	0.00	38.44 (0.43)	0.00	38.53 (0.48)	0.00	37.12 (1.63)	0.00
4 months	0.99 (0.26)	0.00	0.99 (0.26)	0.00	0.77 (0.57)	0.17	0.79 (0.48)	0.09
10 months	1.33 (0.29)	0.00	1.33 (0.29)	0.00	1.25 (0.66)	0.06	1.17 (0.53)	0.03
16 months	1.27 (0.34)	0.00	1.26 (0.34)	0.00	0.92 (0.87)	0.29	1.22 (0.67)	0.07
TG at baseline			0.43 (0.52)	0.41	0.20 (0.60)	0.70	0.45 (0.68)	0.51
TG at 4 months					0.28 (0.71)	0.69	0.51 (0.62)	0.40
TG at 10 months					0.09 (0.83)	0.91	0.31 (0.68)	0.65
TG at 16 months					1.31 (1.07)	0.23	-0.02 (0.83)	0.98
Female							0.69 (0.61)	0.26
Age at baseline							0.01 (0.03)	0.77
Income (percentiles)							0.03 (0.10)	0.75
Random part								
Intercept variance[a] ψ_i	16.05 (1.86)	0.00	16.05 (1.86)	0.00	13.75 (2.02)	0.00	15.10 (2.06)	0.00
Slope variance[b] ψ_s	0.46 (0.24)	0.06	0.46 (0.24)	0.06	2.34 (0.52)	0.00	0.50 (0.27)	0.06
Residual variance[c] θ	5.87 (0.51)	0.00	5.87 (0.51)	0.00	9.55 (0.81)	0.00	5.12 (0.54)	0.00

Table 10. Estimates and standard error (SE) of change in level of physical activity among the TG and the PG. The number of all (both the TG and the PG) participants for the given time points (displayed in chronological sequence) were: n = 267, n = 179, n = 160 and n = 122.

a) Intercept variance represents random deviation from the population mean in initial level of physical activity
b) Slope variance represents random deviation from the population mean of change in level of physical activity
c) Residual variance represents a summary of individual random deviation between the estimated individual trajectory and the true individual score

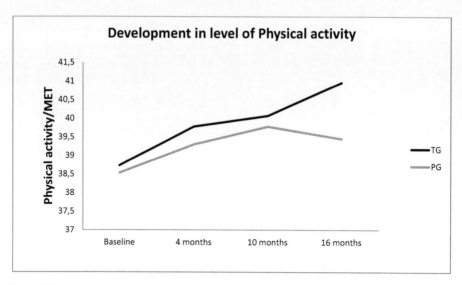

Figure 18: Development in level of physical activity across time points for the TG and the PG. The number of participants for the given time points (displayed in chronological sequence) were: TG: n = 168, n = 114, n = 101 and n = 82; and PG: n = 99, n = 65, n = 59 and n = 40.

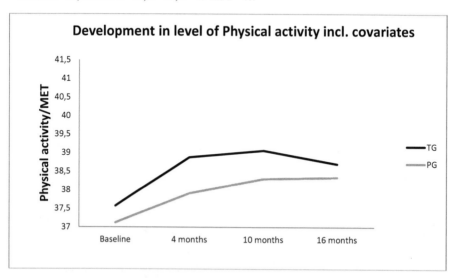

Figure 19: Development in level of physical activity across time points for the TG and the PG after introducing covariates (model 4). The number of participants for the given time points (displayed in chronological sequence) were: TG: n = 108, n = 74, n = 67 and n = 28; and PG: n = 59, n = 50, n = 43 and n = 28.

Physical activity Variables	Odds Ratio	Std. error	Z	p-value	95% Conf. Interval	
Female	1.369	0.966	0.44	0.65	0.343	5.458
Age	1.026	0.368	0.74	0.46	0.957	1.101
Income	0.917	0.110	-0.71	0.48	0.725	1.161
BMI	1.132	0.712	1.98	0.04	1.001	1.280
Education (1)	1.065	0.502	0.13	0.89	0.422	2.683
Education (2)	0.516	0.161	-2.12	0.03	0.279	0.952
Number (n) =	105					
LR chi2(6) =	12.70					
Prob > chi2 =	0.048					
Log likelihood =	-32.969					
Pseudo R2 =	0.162					

Table 11. Logistic regression analysis of missing values at 10 months in relation to levels of physical activity. The table indicates a significantly higher probability for having missing values in relation to physical activity with higher BMI and lower education (2).

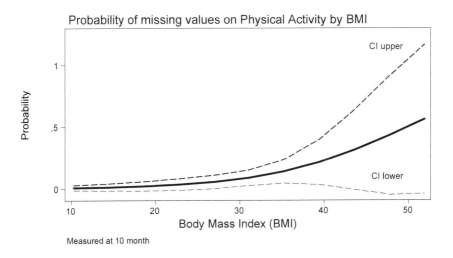

Figure 20. The figure illustrates that the probability of having drop-outs or missing values for levels of physical activity at 10 months increases as BMI increases.

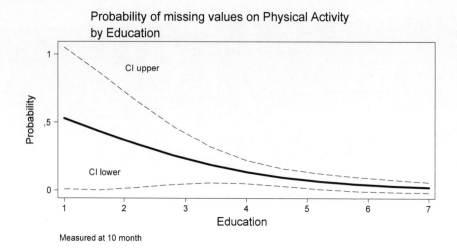

Figure 21. The figure illustrates that the probability of having drop-outs or missing values for levels of physical activity at 10 months increases with decreasing education (2).

Self-efficacy (hypothesis three)

High and low levels of self-efficacy at baseline in regard to levels of physical activity
In this analysis, level of physical activity as the outcome measure in regard to high and low baseline level of *self-efficacy* was included. The measure identifying the two groups of participants with high and low level of *self-efficacy* at baseline was introduced in model 2 of physical activity to investigate for possible differences. Results of the estimates for the grouping variable was observed statistically significant ($\beta = 1.20$, SE = 0.51, p = 0.02), suggesting that the initial level of physical activity at baseline was higher for individuals with high baseline level of *self-efficacy*. In model 3, the possible difference in change in level of physical activity for the two groups at each measurement point in time was investigated. Results from the final model suggested no statistically significant difference in the change in level of physical activity between the groups in regards to level of *self-efficacy* at baseline, 4 and 10 months but a statistically significant difference at 16 months was seen. In general the marginal change in the variance component estimates suggest that the grouping variable does not serve as an important predictor of initial level of physical activity or as a predictor of change in level of physical activity over time. Only at 16 months a difference seems to be apparent (table 12). Figure 22 illustrates development in level of physical activity across all time point for participants (both TG and PG) with high and low level of baseline *self-efficacy* (figure 22).

Furthermore, when the TG and the PG group are analysed separately results show that no statistically significant difference in change of level of physical activity could be seen when comparing groups of high versus low level of baseline *self-efficacy* (table 13). Figure 23 and 24 illustrates development in level of physical activity across all time point for participants in the TG and the PG with high and low level of baseline *self-efficacy* (figure 23 and 24).

77

Variables	Model 1 β (SE)	p-value	Model 2 β (SE)	p-value	Model 3 β (SE)	p-value
Fixed part						
Baseline	38.70 (0.28)	0.00	38.01 (0.39)	0.00	38.11 (0.41)	0.00
4 months	0.99 (0.26)	0.00	0.97 (0.27)	0.00	1.02 (0.40)	0.01
10 months	1.33 (0.29)	0.00	1.31 (0.30)	0.00	1.17 (0.44)	0.01
16 months	1.27 (0.34)	0.00	1.13 (0.35)	0.01	0.37 (0.50)	0.42
High level of self-efficacy at baseline			1.20 (0.51)	0.02	1.03 (0.56)	0.07
High level of self-efficacy at 4 months					-0.07 (0.54)	0.88
High level of self-efficacy at 10 months					0.30 (0.59)	0.63
High level of self-efficacy at 16 months					1.45 (0.68)	0.03
Random part						
Slope variance[b] ψ_s	0.46 (0.24)	0.01	0.49 (0.24)	0.00	0.42 (0.24)	0.07
Intercept variance[a] ψ_i	16.05 (1.85)	0.00	15.86 (1.88)	0.00	15.71 (1.87)	0.00
Residual variance[c] θ	5.87 (0.51)	0.00	5.79 (0.51)	0.00	5.79 (0.51)	0.00

Table 12. Estimates and standard error (SE) of change in level of physical activity among all participants with high versus low level of *self-efficacy* at baseline. The number of all (both the TG and the PG) participants for the given time points (displayed in chronological sequence) were: n = 255, n = 169, n = 148 and n = 116.

a) Intercept variance represents random deviation from the population mean in initial level of physical activity
b) Slope variance represents random deviation from the population mean of change in level of physical activity
c) Residual variance represents a summary of individual random deviation between the estimated individual trajectory and the true individual score

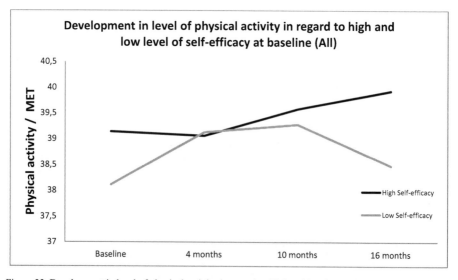

Figure 22. Development in level of physical activity in regard to high and low level of *self-efficacy* at baseline for all participants. The number of participants for the given time points (displayed in chronological sequence) were: High *self-efficacy*: n = 136, n = 90, n = 83 and n = 61; and Low *self-efficacy*: n = 119, n = 79, n = 65 and n = 55.

Variables	TG		PG	
	β (SE)	p-value	β (SE)	p-value
Fixed part				
Baseline	38.40 (0.51)	0.00	37.69 (0.69)	0.00
4 months	0.94 (0.50)	0.06	1.12 (0.63)	0.07
10 months	0.72 (0.58)	0.21	1.70 (0.70)	0.01
16 months	0.52 (0.66)	0.42	0.08 (0.74)	0.92
High level of self-efficacy at baseline	0.56 (0.67)	0.40	1.75 (1.00)	0.08
High level of self-efficacy at 4 months	0.11 (0.66)	0.86	-0.43 (0.90)	0.64
High level of self-efficacy at 10 months	1.04 (0.75)	0.17	-0.93 (0.95)	0.33
High level of self-efficacy at 16 months	1.32 (0.86)	0.13	1.68 (1.11)	0.13
Random part				
Slope variance[b] ψ_s	0.55 (0.29)	0.07	0.15 (0.40)	0.89
Intercept variance[a] ψ_i	13.29 (2.09)	0.00	19.68 (3.06)	0.00
Residual variance[c] θ	5.45 (0.60)	0.00	6.23 (0.92)	0.00

Table 13. Estimates and standard error (SE) of change in level of physical activity among participants with high versus low level of *self-efficacy* at baseline, separated in the TG and the PG.
   a) Intercept variance represents random deviation from the population mean in initial level of physical activity
   b) Slope variance represents random deviation from the population mean of change in physical activity
   c) Residual variance represents a summary of individual random deviation between the estimated individual trajectory and the true individual score

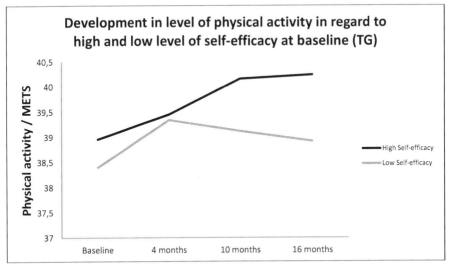

Figure 23. Development in level of physical activity in regard to high and low level of *self-efficacy* at baseline (TG). The number of participants for the given time points (displayed in chronological sequence) were: High *self-efficacy*: n = 91, n = 59, n = 55 and n = 44; and Low *self-efficacy*: n = 69, n = 46, n = 36 and n = 32.

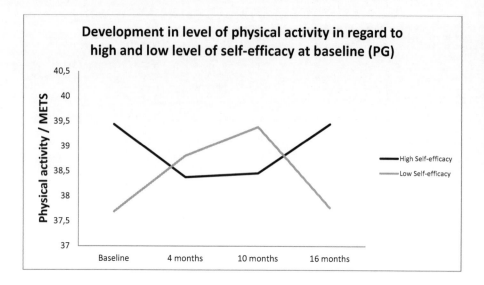

Figure 24. Development in level of physical activity in regard to high and low level of *self-efficacy* at baseline (PG). The number of participants for the given time points (displayed in chronological sequence) were: High *self-efficacy*: n = 45, n = 31, n = 28 and n = 17; and Low *self-efficacy*: n = 50, n = 33, n = 29 and n = 23.

Stages of change (hypothesis three)

High and low level of stage of change at baseline in regard to level of physical activity

In this analysis level of physical activity as the outcome measure in regard to high and low level of baseline *stage of change* was included. The measure identifying the two groups of participants with high and low level of *stage of change* at baseline was introduced in model 2 to investigate for possible differences. Results of the estimates for the grouping variable was observed statistically insignificant ($\beta = 0.12$, SE = 0.56, p = 0.84), suggesting that the initial level of physical activity at baseline was not different for the two groups of participants having high or low level of *stage of change* at baseline. In model 3, the possible difference in change in level of physical activity for the two groups at each measurement point in time was investigated. Results from the final model suggested no statistically significant difference in level of physical activity between the high versus low level of *stage of change* group at any point in time. In general the marginal change in the variance component estimates suggest that the grouping variable in regard to high and low level of *stages of change* does not serve as an important predictor of initial level of physical activity or as a predictor of change in level of physical activity over time (table 14). Figure 25 illustrates development in level of physical activity across all time point for participants (both TG and PG) with high and low level of baseline *stages of change* (figure 25).

Moreover, when the TG and the PG group are analysed separately results show that no statistically significant difference in level of physical activity could be seen in when comparing groups of high versus low baseline level of *self-efficacy* (table 15). Figure 26 and 27 illustrates development in level of physical activity across all time point for participants in TG and PG with high and low baseline level of *stages of change* (figure 26 and 27).

Variables	Model 1		Model 2		Model 3	
	β (SE)	p-value	β (SE)	p-value	β (SE)	p-value
Fixed part						
Baseline	38.49 (0.28)	0.00	38.46 (0.33)	0.00	38.42 (0.34)	0.00
4 months	0.96 (0.27)	0.00	0.96 (0.27)	0.00	1.07 (0.33)	0.00
10 months	1.30 (0.30)	0.00	1.30 (0.30)	0.00	1.26 (0.36)	0.00
16 months	1.40 (0.35)	0.00	1.40 (0.35)	0.00	1.66 (0.44)	0.00
High level of stages of change at baseline			0.12 (0.56)	0.84	0.23 (0.61)	0.70
High level of stages of change at 4 months					-0.33 (0.57)	0.55
High level of stages of change at 10 months					0.16 (0.64)	0.81
High level of stages of change at 16 months					-0.77 (0.75)	0.30
Random part						
Slope variance[b] ψ_s	0.56 (0.25)	0.01	0.56 (0.25)	0.01	0.58 (0.25)	0.01
Intercept variance[a] ψ_i	14.87 (1.79)	0.00	14.86 (1.79)	0.00	14.92 (1.80)	0.00
Residual variance[c] θ	5.58 (0.50)	0.00	5.58 (0.51)	0.00	5.55 (0.50)	0.00

Table 14. Estimates and standard error (SE) of change in level of physical activity among participants with high versus low level of *stages of change* at baseline. The number of all (both the TG and the PG) participants for the given time points (displayed in chronological sequence) were: n = 245, n = 163, n = 142 and n = 111.
   a) Intercept variance represents random deviation from the population mean in initial level of physical activity
   b) Slope variance represents random deviation from the population mean of change in physical activity
   c) Residual variance represents a summary of individual random deviation between the estimated individual trajectory and the true individual score

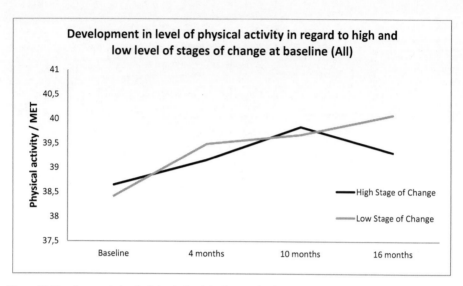

Figure 25. Development in level of physical activity in regard to high and low level of *stages of change* at baseline for all participants. The number of participants for the given time points (displayed in chronological sequence) were: High *stages of change*: n = 168, n = 109, n = 97 and n = 72; and Low *stages of change*: n = 77, n = 54, n = 45 and n = 39.

Variables	TG		PG	
	β (SE)	p-value	β (SE)	p-value
Fixed part				
Baseline	38.59 (0.41)	0.00	38.17 (0.58)	0.00
4 months	0.93 (0.41)	0.02	1.26 (0.53)	0.02
10 months	1.07 (0.47)	0.02	1.38 (0.55)	0.01
16 months	1.87 (0.56)	0.00	1.08 (0.66)	0.10
High level of stages of change at baseline	-0.00 (0.69)	0.99	0.65 (1.16)	0.58
High level of stages of change at 4 months	0.22 (0.66)	0.74	-1.66 (1.08)	0.12
High level of stages of change at 10 months	0.32 (0.78)	0.69	0.03 (1.14)	0.98
High level of stages of change at 16 months	-0.74 (0.91)	0.41	-0.85 (1.29)	0.51
Random part				
Slope variance[b] ψ_s	0.71 (0.30)	0.01	0.20 (0.41)	0.90
Intercept variance[a] ψ_i	12.10 (1.93)	0.00	19.09 (3.57)	0.00
Residual variance[c] θ	5.09 (0.57)	0.00	6.28 (0.93)	0.00

Table 15. Estimates and standard error (SE) of change in level of physical activity among participants with high versus low level of *stages of change* at baseline, separated in the TG and the PG
   a) Intercept variance represents random deviation from the population mean in initial level of physical activity
   b) Slope variance represents random deviation from the population mean of change in physical activity
   c) Residual variance represents a summary of individual random deviation between the estimated individual trajectory and the true individual score

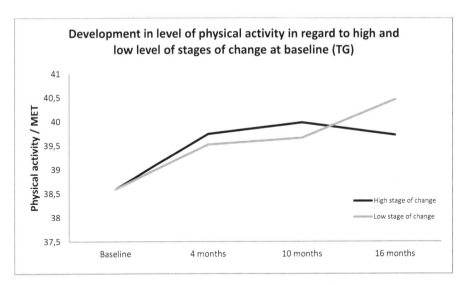

Figure 26. Development in level of physical activity in regard to high and low level of *stages of change* at baseline (TG). The number of participants for the given time points (displayed in chronological sequence) were: High *stages of change*: n = 98, n = 63, n = 54 and n = 44; and Low *stages of change*: n = 54, n = 39, n = 31 and n = 28.

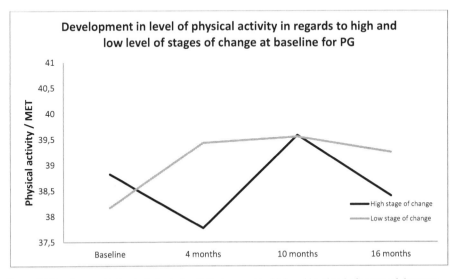

Figure 27. Development in level of physical activity in regard to high and low level of *stages of change* at baseline (PG). The number of participants for the given time points (displayed in chronological sequence) were: High *stages of change*: n = 70, n = 46, n = 43 and n = 28; and Low *stages of change*: n = 23, n = 15, n = 14 and n = 11.

Qualitative results

As mentioned earlier, the aim of the qualitative study was to substantiate, elaborate and supplement the quantitative data in relation to the hypotheses, and furthermore explore hypothesis four (Fox et al., 2007). The interviews were conducted to explore possible additional factors that influence *self-efficacy*, *stages of change*, physical activity and the hypotheses. The findings from the interview study are reported in the following order: *self-efficacy*, *stages of change*, and physical activity, and in relation to the hypotheses.

Self-efficacy

One goal of the interviews was to explore *self-efficacy* in relation to experienced barriers and the degree to which the informants in the TG and the PG were assumed to be able to be physically active in spite of these (Benisovich et al., 1998; Marcus et al., 1992b). Furthermore, the interviews explored possible facilitating conditions towards physical activity.

In relation to hypothesis one, there were no apparent long-term changes in *self-efficacy* towards barriers for participants in the TG or the PG. In the TG, barriers such as bodily discomfort, lack of inclination to exercise, time, transport and practical issues and minimal effects from the intervention were reported as important barriers at all measurement points. They were reported without any indication of *self-efficacy* towards these barriers being decisively altered across time. New barriers even seemed to appear when the informants were challenged to be physically active on their own.

> *The physical and especially the psychological tiredness from some kind of symptom in my body is a barrier (informant TG).*

> *I must admit that I have not felt like exercising for a while because the things which make exercising all right are missing (e.g., the competitive challenge and the social element) (informant TG).*

In the TG, the high intensity training programme and the motivational counselling only seem to affect the way the informants articulate their barriers during and immediately after the intense intervention. The training and motivational counselling do not seem to affect *self-efficacy* of overcoming barriers in the long-term.

> *Of course you should be able to take care of yourself after the TG. Nobody else holds your hand in your everyday life, but in the TG I think I needed some more follow-up (informant TG).*

Participants in the PG experienced barriers similar to the TG participants. The informants reported the main barriers were: lack of prioritisation of physical activity, time, transport, practical issues, as well as other participants. Furthermore, barriers related to uncertainty of physical competence, social relations, environment and economy were also mentioned. The PG informants primarily seemed to differ from informants in the TG by not describing bodily illness or pain as a problem. In spite of *self-efficacy* in relation to these barriers not being altered, the PG informants seemed to increase or maintain their physical activity level, whereas the TG informants seemed to decrease their activity or became totally inactive according to long-term analyses.

> *If I went somewhere to exercise, then they would think, she is not competent doing this. I would feel stupid and inadequate (informant PG).*

> *We had to do exercises in groups and pairs and it was not for me. I have to exercise with someone I know (informant PG).*

In essence, the informants in both the TG and the PG seem to indicate the same barriers towards exercise and give the same expression about their *self-efficacy* towards these barriers. The recurring barriers for both groups could be summarised as: lack of interest in physical activity, difficulty finding the right place to exercise, exercise taking important time away from everyday chores, being a single mother, time spent on transport to and from activities and not being able to make time to exercise. Otherwise, the primary barriers to becoming physically active were very different from individual to individual.

> *It is a barrier if I have to join anything scheduled. I would like to do things that interest me more than physical activity (informant PG).*

> *I do not like to be in changing rooms with a lot of sweaty people, I know I am a bit peculiar. I do not want to be on those floors near smelly mats; I just cannot do it (informant PG).*

The limitation of movement due to lifestyle diseases and physical discomfort expressed by informants in the TG is an exception to the homogenous statements of the informants in both groups. This barrier seems to be recurring and especially essential. The bodily condition and the derived *self-efficacy* thoughts seem to be especially inhibitory of changing towards a more physically active behaviour.

> *It hurts to exercise. I get medication to ease the pain when I am exercising. That is not fun. It is really a hurdle to overcome. It gives me too many excuses for not exercising (informant TG).*

In terms of hypotheses two and three, the informants in both groups at baseline are convinced about their ability to overcome major barriers and become physically active, which indicates relatively high *self-efficacy* in relation to barriers. Still, differences between the two groups seem to be apparent. The TG informants seem to express an increased optimism in overcoming barriers compared to the PG informants. At baseline, they are convinced they can overcome their barriers because they have become a part of a structured intervention in which things (e.g. training and counselling) are organised for them. They feel privileged but also obliged to make an effort. The informants in the PG do not seem to feel obliged in the same way. They are not part of a structured intervention and have ambivalent thoughts concerning their own abilities to overcome barriers.

> *I do not think you can get the opportunity to be a part of an intervention and then just stop. It gives me a greater sense of obligation. I have no right to stop (informant TG).*

> *I was happy to be able to participate. I have accepted all their offers. When they have saved your life and then offer you an intervention, it is almost impossible to decline (informant TG).*

> *I am not convinced that I can be physically active. If I have to join anything scheduled it is a barrier (informant PG).*

Thus, the initial *self-efficacy* in relation to barriers seems to be higher for members of the TG group than for the PG group members. This is primarily due to the TG group members' inclusion in a structured intervention, where the responsibility is placed on others, not on themselves. However, according to the analyses of hypothesis one in both the quantitative and the qualitative studies, this initial difference in *self-efficacy* does not influence overcoming barriers in the long run or increase adherence to physically active behaviour.

To explore further the area of *self-efficacy*, the informants were asked if they were aware of any facilitating conditions which could help them become physically active and/or enhance their *self-efficacy*. As with the barriers, the participants in both interventions were aware of facilitating factors which could help them in their efforts to become physically active. Helpful initiatives seemed primarily to be individually determined, but reduced working hours and flexibility on the job were two consistent factors considered to be helpful for becoming physically active. Increased help from the exercise specialist, easier accessibility to exercise, more spare time to exercise, help from social relations and individually adjusted and varied exercise programmes were also repeated as facilitators in both groups.

If I am honest, then I think reduced working hours would help me. It sounds crazy, but to have a whole day off to do things you want without having a guilty conscience would be fantastic (informant TG).

Other facilitating conditions mentioned as important to increasing physical activity were exercising with friends and family, having a guilty conscience, a clear knowledge of what the physical effort will lead to (e.g., increased amount of instruction) and feedback from measurement tools (e.g., pedometer, body fat tool).

I thrive when I am committed to somebody. I do best in the company of others (informant TG).

I have bought an instrument to measure fat. It is quite essential. I have bought these types of instruments because they interest me a lot. They will help me stay motivated (informant PG).

One facilitating factor mentioned right after the intervention, but also at long-term, especially by the informants in the TG, was witnessing their health improve and physical capacity increase. Such an improvement was expressed as helpful for staying motivated and doing physical activities.

It is a pleasure for me to go to the fitness centre. It is because I feel physical progress and still learn something new...I will continue to strive after the goals I decided on with help from the exercise specialist. When I reach those goals I will be happy. I will tell myself, "now I am normal" (informant PG).

In summary, the informants from both interventions indicated many of the same facilitating conditions at long-term as they did at earlier time-points, but some informants also gained new knowledge of helpful initiatives. Challenge and variation in training programmes, pleasant training environments plus commitment and obligation towards training groups and other participants were mentioned as facilitating exercise behaviour. Even though, being aware of facilitating factors and discovering new helpful initiatives it does not seem to effect adaptation of a physically active lifestyle in long-term.

If I do not feel challenged, I do not feel motivated. I tried exercising in two centres but I got bored with their programmes. I do not think those two places were able to design a programme to match my interest, something was missing (informant TG).

I need to exercise on a team, which is more binding than if I had to do it on my own. I need to be forced to go. If I have committed myself to something I will do it (informant TG).

Given the fact that the informants expressed knowledge about barriers and facilitators and intention to work constructively to overcome the barriers, it is surprising that the majority of the barriers still exist 12 months after intervention and most of them just as strong. This indicates a contradiction between expectancy of outcome and effort needed to reach expected activity level (Jones et al., 2005). It seems that neither training plus motivational counselling or motivational counselling alone are effective enough to process fundamental issues of *self-efficacy* towards barriers. Other factors must influence their ability to change as well.

Exercise is still an obligation. I keep expecting that the benefit will exceed the effort, but I find that hard to imagine (informant TG).

Stages of change

One goal of the interviews was to explore the hypothesised expected development of *stages of change* during and after the intervention, and moreover, to determine if differences in baseline *stages of change* were apparent between the members of the TG and the PG group. Furthermore, another goal was to determine to what extent this possible difference would influence adherence to a physically active lifestyle. To provide a better overview of interview data, results of baseline levels of *stages of change* and differences between groups (related to hypotheses two and three) are presented first. Afterwards, the long-term development of *stages and change* and its effect on physical activity (related to hypothesis one) are presented.

In relation to hypotheses two and three, the basis of *stages of change* was explored at baseline. All of the participants in the TG were referred by their GPs as a result of a regular consultation, and therefore they were suspected to be expecting to receive an ordinary prescription for medication – not exercise. Because of this, the hypothesis was that they would be less ready to change than would be the PG participants, who were included on their own initiative. This prediction was contradicted by statements from the informants suggesting that the initiative, also from the TG informants, to participate in the intervention came from themselves, and not their GPs.

I read about it in the paper and at one point I said: "I am going to call my GP to see if he knows anything about this". He did not know much, so it was actually by my request (informant TG).

Originally, some of the informants in the PG wanted to be a part of the TG because they thought they needed to do something about their physical health. They addressed their GPs to get a prescription, but were referred to the PG because they did not meet the inclusion criteria.

In general, small differences in *stages of change* were apparent between the informants in the TG and the PG at baseline. The results from the interview study indicated, that the informants in the TG were found to be in the "preparation stage" and the "action stage", based on their answers indicating that they were preparing to start exercising (e.g. making initial contact to a fitness centre or buying running shoes) or already had started exercising. The informants in the PG, on the other hand, indicated different initial *stages of change*. These informants were categorised as belonging to the "contemplation", "preparation" and "action" stages (table 16).

Informant	Project	Change Stage (Baseline)	Short term (4 months)	Longterm (10 months)	Long-term (16 months)	Stage progress*
1	TG	Action	Preparation	Action	Contemplation	-2
2	TG	Preparation	Action	Action	Contemplation	-1
3	TG	Preparation	Contemplation	Action	Preparation	0
4	TG	Preparation	Contemplation	Contemplation	Contemplation	-1
5	PG	Action	Action	Action	Maintenance	+1
6	PG	Preparation	Action	Action	Maintenance	+2
7	PG	Contemplation	Preparation	Preparation	Action	+2

Table 16. Stage distribution and development in *stages of change* at baseline, 4, 10 and 16 months of the informants in the TG and the PG. *The numbers indicated in "Stage progress" indicate the number of progressed stages for the informants. If a negative number is present relapse to earlier stages are current.

In relation to hypothesis one, the interview data uncover the dynamics of the informants' progression through the stages. Firstly, results from the TG are presented and then results from the PG.

Immediately after the intervention (4 months), only one of four informants in the TG had progressed positively through stages, whereas three had relapsed and were now physically inactive, or contemplating or preparing (table 16). The active informant exercises because she feels obliged to improve her physical condition.

> *I do it because I feel obliged to get exercise, but I have not noticed any extreme changes in my physique (informant TG).*

However, six months after the intervention, three of four informants in the TG had succeeded in becoming regularly physically active. However, the informants' attitudes towards exercise had not changed. Exercise was still considered an obligation and participation as a necessity for preventing physical degradation. Nevertheless, motivation and enthusiasm were felt and experienced as well.

> *I still exercise from a sense of duty. I feel obliged to exercise and I feel like I have to do it because I joined the TG (informant TG).*

> *I have seldom experienced this kind of enthusiasm as is apparent here (informant TG).*

Subsequent, 16 month after initiation of the intervention, all four informants in the TG were inactive, contemplating or preparing. Physiological explanations and practical issues were given as primary reasons for not being physically active.

> *Seen from an exercise point of view it is worse. We (my GP and I) are not able to locate where this tiredness is coming from right now, but they are checking my medication. My life seems to be in the doldrums, where I, to be honest, do nothing, nothing physical at least (informant TG).*

> *I was planning to start at the fitness centre but I have not come any further because we have been busy with work and school. I think I will wait until we have moved (informant TG).*

On the other hand, the informants in the PG seem to have a more persistent progression through the stages. Basically, a positive progression through the stages can be seen for all of the informants in the PG. All informants in the PG manage to become more physically active over the long-term. Two informants even manage to sustain their physical activity long enough to be categorised in the "maintenance" stage (table 16).

Immediately after the intervention, all informants in the PG had increased their amount of physical activity. The increase in physical activity had occurred primarily by increasing everyday activities (e.g., walking) and only on one occasion by making concrete plans for doing fitness exercise.

> *I have not had the resources to start up exercising as fast as I had expected. I had expected to be roller skating and training at a fitness centre by now (informant PG).*

After 10 months, two of three informants in the PG had maintained their physical activity level, whereas one informant was still in the preparation stage. At this point, different attitudes existed between the informants. One informant found exercising to be a waste of time and the cause of her back pain. Another informant felt that physical activity was motivating and had integrated exercising as a structured part of his life. One informant was still located in the preparation stage primarily due to her social barriers towards other participants (table 16). Subsequently, 16 months after initiation of the intervention, the informants in the PG had succeeded in staying physically active. They had managed to generate more time and motivation to exercise regularly.

> *I work out more. It seems like I have more time to do it and I think you need to take care of yourself; you have to do something (informant PG).*

> *I walk at least thirty minutes. I have become more energetic riding my bike into town as well (informant PG).*

The results indicate, that the PG informants had greater success in becoming physically active than did the TG informants (table 16). Long-term adherence to physical activity is an important aim of participation in Exercise on Prescription, but in essence, no real persistent progression through the stages can be seen for the four informants from the TG. It seems as if they are dynamically moving back and forth through stages without any real long-term adherence to physical activity, and relapse to earlier *stages of change* seems to be apparent (table 16).

In addition to information about stage progress, the analysis of *stages of change* indicated interesting new findings. As predicted by the hypotheses, the initial placement in *stages of change* was suspected to be important or decisive in predicting long-term behaviour change in both groups. In contrast to this, the results showed that an initial high level of *stage of change* was not critical. The type of attitude towards physical activity and exercise seemed to be a more important characteristic for successful long-term adherence to physical activity. The incentive to participate at baseline, as well as 16 months after initiation of the intervention, seemed to be different for the two groups.

Statements from informants in the TG suggest that their participation in the TG and physical activity in general were facilitated by a critical need to change their lifestyles, a fear of dying from their diseases and an obligation towards themselves, their family and the intervention. Their attitudes and motivation towards participating in the intervention were primarily influenced by a conception of themselves exercising due to an obligation to prevent getting seriously ill or dying from their diseases. Overall, they did not participate because they were motivated to do or interested in physical activity.

> *I have heart problems and I think I use too much medication. I am becoming fatter and fatter, more and more tired and drained of energy and my body progressively hurts more. I think it was really bad and I had to do something, I had to pull myself up by my bootstraps. I participate because I have to (informant TG).*

In contrast to this, the informants from the PG seem to express interest and motivation to become more physically active to alter their well being in everyday life. It seems like the PG informants are using the intervention as an aid to pursue individual goals of becoming healthier.

Social Relations

The influence of social relations is investigated in relation to hypothesis four, to determine if specific social relations influence and facilitate physical activity behaviour or whether the same social relations limit adherence to physical activity. In this study, social relations are defined as family (spouse and children) and friends, the general practitioner, the exercise specialist and other participants in the intervention.

Family and Friends

In general, family were reported as being influential in regards to exercise behaviour and adherence to a physically active lifestyle after intervention for members of both groups. A supportive family environment was stated as facilitating and conducive for adherence, whereas being a single mother seemed to impede increased exercise behaviour.

> *She (daughter) slows down a part of my life. I have nobody who is able to take care of her yet. It slows me down a little and that irritates me (informant TG).*

> *My family means a lot to me. If I had to choose between exercise and being with my friends and family, I would choose them over exercise (informant PG).*

In relation to friends, the interviewed informants stated that a close-knit behavioural pattern amongst friends can be a barrier for behaviour change. Furthermore, none of the informants had friends who exercised on a regular basis, and when they spent time together, other issues like education, culture, wine and food were discussed.

> *You do not change your social relations and when you try to change your behaviour they notice it. In the beginning it is cool to be different, but after a few months seeing the same people, you have returned to your old habits (informant PG).*

> *I do not spend time with my friends to exercise. It is the social aspect which is important (informant TG).*

General practitioner

It was hypothesised that the general practitioner is a key person in motivating and influencing the participants (Camaione et al., 1997; McKenna & Vernon, 2004). The GP had contact with the participants in the TG and the PG, and wrote the referral to the TG or sent participants to the PG if they did not meet the inclusion criteria of the TG. Surprisingly, none of the informants in the TG or the PG considered the GP as important in their decisions to participate. Furthermore, they stated that their GP did not know much about the intervention besides their ability to give the referral.

> *We only talked about it when I talked with her about getting started exercising. Neither my old nor my new GP has mentioned the PG. It is like they have no interest in it. But at the same time they tell me to do something to help myself (informant PG).*

They considered the GP to be a peripheral person with no impact on their behaviour. Apart from their initial visit at the GP and referral to the TG or the PG, the informants state that they have had no further contact with their GP in relation to the interventions.

> *No, I have not had any talks with my GP concerning the TG subsequently. She sees me once a month concerning my blood pressure (informant TG).*

Neither the informants in the PG or the TG have experienced their GP as a supportive, motivating or influential person in relation to the intervention. They find that the GP is concerned about physiological issues and not participation or adherence to physical activity.

Exercise Specialist

Informants in both groups made different statements about the exercise specialist. Some informants found the role of the exercise specialist very important, motivating and a great influence on their behavioural change process. They felt the amount of motivational counselling and contact with the exercise specialist was important. Some even appointed the success of their adherence to the exercise specialist.

> *The exercise specialist has made me think about exercising. Her behaviour is catching; she seems inspiring. I do not know if it has made me change my behaviour but at any rate it has made me maintain a conception of exercise as important (informant TG).*

> *I think the conversations have been really constructive, positive and optimistic. The basis of our conversation has been my thoughts concerning motivation and planning. She does the things I have difficulty doing like making initial contact. She has made it possible for me to get started (informant PG).*

Others stated that their consultations with the exercise specialist were a waste of time. They did not find the guidance and suggestions from the exercise specialist useful or suitable for their situation.

> *The exercise specialist has not convinced me of anything and she has not influenced my decision concerning exercising in any way. I had from the beginning decided what to do. I talked to her earlier, but I did not think she could offer me anything useful (informant TG).*

16 months after initiation of the intervention, several of the informants stated that they would have preferred the exercise specialist's counselling to last for a longer period to help them adhere to their exercise behaviours.

Other participants in the TG and the PG

In general, the informants in the TG and the PG discussed the role of the other participants in two different ways. Firstly, the other participants were described as an essential network within which the informants could feel secure because of the homogeneity of the group. The support from the group and the obligation towards the other participants were indicated as important factors for helping the informants stay physically active.

> *If you are part of a group then you are responsible for it; that is obvious. If you start with fourteen people, you will have to be fourteen people every time, otherwise the group will shut down. You have a social obligation to be there (informant TG).*

To exercise alone would not affect me the same way as exercising in a group. My expectations are for the others to be supportive and to motivate me to participate, but I do not participate for social reasons. I think it is all right to say that I do it only for me (informant TG).

In contrast to these experiences, the other participants could also be seen as barriers, limiting and intimidating. Explanations included that the informants did not feel a sense of connectedness with the others, a general resistance towards being part of a larger group or disliking being with other sweaty, malodorous people.

We do not mean anything to each other. If we should try to build social relations in the group, I am not the one to contribute. I am dressed when I arrive and leave immediately after exercise. Nobody from the TG will leave lasting impressions in my mind (informant TG).

I think of them as indolent, at least it is the way I perceive them. It was the same way I perceived myself when my GP suggested the TG – an intervention for indolent people (informant TG).

Overall, family was indicated as the strongest facilitator or barrier. The exercise specialist like other participants could be a motivating and effective key persons as well as discouraging, whereas the GP was described as without significance.

Discussion

In the following section, discussion of the results will be separated in the discussion of the quantitative results followed by the qualitative results. The results will be discussed in relation to the hypotheses and presented in the following order: *self-efficacy*, *stages of change* and physical activity.

Quantitative results

Self-efficacy

In relation to hypothesis one, the level of *self-efficacy* did not change in either group throughout the study period. This is in contradiction with research showing a positive development in level of *self-efficacy* with participation in an intervention (Jones et al., 2005) and an association between an increased level of physical activity (physical activity results) and increased level of *self-efficacy* (Cardinal & Kosma, 2004; Edmunds et al., 2008; Marcus et al., 1992b; McAuley, 1993). Consistent with the arguments offered by Jones et al. (2005), participation throughout the programme reflects individual motivation regardless of group characteristics. Thus, it is possible that self-selection resulted in a sample that was homogeneous with regard to level of *self-efficacy*.

Since the current results show a significant development in level of physical activity over time, the impact of the intervention on *self-efficacy* level could be debated. One explanation for the lack of development in levels of *self-efficacy* in the TG could possibly be the transition from the structured intervention programme to unassisted training after 4 months. This transition from one organisational form to another could be described as a key element of the TG intervention. The TG informants cross from a structured programme, where others are responsible, to unassisted physical activity of their own responsibility. This change of responsibility could affect the TG members' level of *self-efficacy* to such a degree that development in *self-efficacy* level fails to happen. This indicates that the motivational counselling and the intervention are not effective enough to process this fundamental issue. This is not relevant for the PG since no organisational change happens. This also indicates that the TG intervention in spite of a more intense intervention is not more effective in influencing levels of *self-efficacy* and thereby levels of physical activity. This is supported by literature showing no difference in level of *self-efficacy* between control group members and intervention group members (van Sluijs et al., 2005a).

In relation to hypothesis two, it could be hypothesised that deciding to be a part of an intervention illustrates interest and motivation and therefore possibly a high level of *self-efficacy* towards barriers. This is consistent with literature showing motivation or interest as an important incentive for being physically active (Biddle & Mutrie, 2007) and literature indicating that level of *self-efficacy* is a significant predictor of exercise behaviour in the early and middle stages of an exercise program (McAuley et al., 1994). Therefore, it was initially hypothesised that the PG would score higher in level of *self-efficacy* at baseline than the TG because they volunteered to be a part of the intervention, instead of being referred by their GPs. The results do not support this hypothesis; the initial level of *self-efficacy* concerning barriers was the same for both groups. Major barriers (e.g., motivation or having an illness and injury) are described in the literature as important in the initial change towards physical activity (Sallis & Hovell, 1990). Acknowledging this, the participants in the TG could possibly have greater barriers towards being physically active due to their lifestyle diseases and as a consequence of this a lower level of *self-efficacy*. Unfortunately, specific information about the participants' lifestyle diseases was not available. A thorough analysis including this information could possibly provide knowledge indicating whether certain lifestyle diseases are more hampering for the development of lifestyle diseases than others. This information could possibly have improved the effort of practitioners and organisers to influence levels of *self-efficacy*.

In relation to hypotheses one and two, one could question whether the results of the analyses can be trusted due to the comparison of two different groups receiving two different interventions. Since baseline differences between the groups, introduced as covariates in analyses, did not statistically significantly influence the results, the results could be trusted to the extent the strengths of the design permit. Possible bias could be found in areas other than gender, age, BMI, education and income. Future analyses, for example, could include information on health status and lifestyle diseases at baseline as potential factors biasing results. Another issue that should be addressed is the high degree of drop-outs in both groups, and how this might bias the finding concerning levels of *self-efficacy*; however, since drop-out analyses did not influence the results significantly, factors other than drop-outs may be more important in explaining the lack of development in levels of *self-efficacy*.

In relation to hypothesis three, the results indicate that when we dichotomise baseline levels of *self-efficacy* (high and low) for all participants, the group with a high level of *self-efficacy* had a statistically significantly greater level of physical activity at baseline. This, as mentioned earlier, is supported by literature showing an association between level of *self-efficacy* and level of physical activity (McAuley et al., 1994). When investigating differences in changes in level of physical activity for the high and low *self-efficacy* groups for each measurement point in time, results showed no statistically significant differences in the change in level of physical activity between the groups at 4 and 10 months, but a statistically significant difference at 16 months This difference corresponds to an increase of approximately 1.5 MET or 20-30 minutes of walking a day. A change of 1 MET per day, is shown in research to be equivalent to walking an extra 10-15 minutes (Ainsworth et al., 2000). But when the TG and the PG are analysed separately, results showed that no statistically significant difference in level of physical activity could be seen when comparing groups of high versus low baseline level of *self-efficacy*. This indicates that a high level of *self-efficacy* is not related to the intervention itself (van Sluijs et al., 2005a) but to the individual. This is underlined by analyses of baseline differences between the TG and the PG showing differences not to influence neither level of *self-efficacy* or level of physical activity.

Stages of change

In relation to hypothesis one, the results indicated, as hypothesised, that the probability of a high level of *stage of change* increased in both the TG and the PG over time. Thus, the findings are consistent with observations reported by Kallings (2008) (Kallings et al., 2008) and with literature indicating progression in level of *stages of change* to be related to progression in intervention and physical activity (Biddle & Mutrie, 2007). Moreover, these results are supported by literature indicating no differences in *stage of change* between volunteers and recruited participants to health promotion programs (Prochaska & Velicer, 1997). However, a study debates the applicability when measuring mild exercise, which in most cases is current in the TG and PG (Schumann et al., 2003).

In relation to hypothesis two, the results suggest, in contrast to predictions that the participants in both groups exhibited about the same initial levels of *stages of change*. This is surprising since the members of the PG group were expected to have progressed further in their initial level of *stage of change* than the TG members since participation was voluntary (Biddle & Mutrie, 2007). The lack of differences in level of *stages of change* between the TG and PG may be explained by the dichotomisation of the measure of *stages of change* into high and low levels. Finely graded differences between the groups, with regard to variations in distinct stages, are possibly blurred by the reduction of six stages into two (Nigg, 2002). Nonetheless, the results still suggest that the participants moved progressively through stages. However, the lack of a statistically significantly difference in probability of high level of *stages of change* between the groups suggests that the distinction between counselling with accompanying training and counselling only did not contribute to the observed overall increase in probability of a high level of *stages of change*.

In relation to hypotheses one and two, as with *self-efficacy*, one might question whether the results of the analyses of levels of *stages of change* can be trusted due to comparing two different groups receiving two different interventions. But since baseline differences did not significantly influence the results of the LGC analyses when introduced as covariates, the results are reliable and relevant in the discussion of the effect of the TG and the PG. Possible bias blurring differences between the groups should be found in areas other than gender, age, BMI, education and income. Furthermore, the high drop-out rate did not influence the results significantly, thereby indicating that factors other than drop-outs may be more important in explaining the lack of development in levels of *self-efficacy*.

In relation to hypothesis three, the analyses of the influence of baseline high and low levels of *stages of change* on levels of physical activity indicated no statistically significant differences between the groups at any measurement point in time. When the TG and the PG group are analysed separately results show that no statistically significant difference in level of physical activity could be seen when comparing groups of high versus low baseline level of *stage of change*.

Physical activity

In relation to hypothesis one, a small positive and statistically significant increase in level of physical activity across the subsequent measurement points in time for both groups was seen. This small yet significant effect on physical activity level in both groups is supported by other studies of *prescribed exercise* showing only moderately positive (Roessler & Ibsen, 2009) or no effect on physical activity level (Dugdill et al., 2005; Harrison et al., 2005b; Hillsdon et al., 2005; Sorensen et al., 2006). In regards to hypothesis one, it could expected that the level of physical activity reported by the TG (receiving training as well as counselling) would be higher compared to the PG (receiving counselling only). Surprisingly, no statistically significant difference between the TG and the PG was observed throughout the study period. These results are contradicted by studies showing greater effects of *prescribed exercise* interventions for treatment groups than controls (Aittasalo et al., 2006), but also supported by a study showing the same effect of counselling on level of physical activity as training, in combination with counselling both at short- and at long-term (Sorensen et al., 2008). The effect of counselling on physical activity level is supported by an earlier study (Elley et al., 2003). Baseline differences between the TG and the PG group introduced as covariates did not alter the results and neither did drop-out analyses. This indicates that factors other than group belonging and the selected socio-demographic factors are determining progress in levels of physical activity.

In general, the results of the present analyses indicate an increasingly higher probability of having a high level of *stages of change* and an increase in level of physical activity from baseline to 16 months. However, changes in these features were indistinguishable between participants in the TG and the PG. No statistically significant differences in level of *self-efficacy* across all measurements point in time were observed. The results of the analyses suggest that the variability of the measures of initial levels and rates of change across time remained the same, suggesting that other factors that characterise the participants may be better predictors of the changes in the outcome than group membership. An important difference between the participants could be the manifest diagnosis among the members of the TG. Obviously, chronic diseases may limit participants physically and mentally and hamper their efforts to fully benefit from the intervention. In future studies and evaluations of Exercise on Prescription, it is necessary to include specific knowledge of the participants' lifestyle diseases to investigate if specific lifestyle diseases hamper adoption of a physically active lifestyle. Future research should investigate this issue in greater depth.

The residual variance remained unchanged in analyses including *self-efficacy*, *stages of change*, and physical activity as the outcome measures. The fact that the intra-individual variances were observed to be statistically significantly different from zero suggests that the measures of the outcome obtained on four occasions across 16 months were unstable. The source of this instability was not investigated, and it is acknowledged that it may be difficult to disentangle the various sources. Thus, it is not known if the instability is caused by poor measurement techniques or true variability in response patterns among the participants or a combination of both.

Bias, imprecision and strengths

Bias and imprecision

The study was designed as a practise based evaluation rather than a controlled trial. This could result in optimistic estimates of the effects of the intervention. The fact that two different groups received two different interventions is problematic. The Hawthorne effect may also cause respondents to provide better responses long-term than they did in the baseline assessment because of general support of the programme, familiarity with the questionnaires and awareness of the relationship between health and physical activity (O'Sullivan et al., 2004). Moreover, the physiotherapists, the exercise specialists, the motivational counsellors and the participants were not blinded to which intervention they were included in or what the aim of the intervention was. This could possibly have resulted in a social desirability bias and consequently a tendency to positively overestimate self-reported results (Adams et al., 2005; Motl et al., 2005). There may also be considerable selection bias among the participants who chose to take part in the study. Several factors can possibly bias the selection. This could e.g. be the general practitioners having to make an assessment of the likelihood that patients would engage in *prescribed exercise* and their willingness to pay the participation fee at time of the referral. To be included in the study the referred patients should also be able and willing to comply with the described data collection and be willing to spend time in follow-up counselling sessions. The sample of participants will therefore not be representative for all individuals who were referred to the *prescribed exercise* intervention or who potentially might benefit from more physical activity. Furthermore, it is not known to what extent the participants in the PhD study differ from the participants included in the overall EoP intervention in Funen County and Frederiksberg Municipality. If the type and/or severity of the lifestyle diseases are different for the participants in the PhD study and participants in the overall EoP intervention, this could bias the results. Unfortunately, these data on lifestyle disease were not obtainable.

Drop-outs also potentially can influence the results. Already at the point when the GP is involved, patients meeting inclusion criteria are deselected due to the GP's assessment. Furthermore, about 50 percent of those receiving a prescription never accept the EoP offer (Roessler & Ibsen, 2009). This introduces additional bias, potentially including a group of participants in the EoP which differs substantially from those not being referred or those choosing not to participate. The results of the PhD study were also influenced by a high drop-out rate. About 55% of the participants initially

101

included in the study answered the questionnaire at 16 months revealing an average drop-out rate of 45%. Even though analyses indicated that drop-outs did not influence the results significantly, it is still possible that those who choose to be a part of the study and complete all four questionnaires could be different from those who drop-out in areas other than the ones analysed. Literature supports drop-outs being different from those who adhere (Jones et al., 2005; Lakerveld et al., 2008). The analyses would have been strengthened if information on individuals deselected by the GPs, those choosing not to participate and additional information on those who dropped out during the intervention had been included. But due to the organisation of the EoP and the design of the PhD study, this information was not available.

Another limitation is the use of self-reported measures. For example, self-reported physical activity may be less accurate than administered methods of doubly labelled water (Ainslie et al., 2003; Conway et al., 2002a; Staten et al., 2001) accelerometers and pedometers (Conway et al., 2002b). However, self-report questionnaires are applicable and easy to administer, and are especially useful in larger studies (Rennie & Wareham, 1998). Additionally, another important issue is whether the questionnaires used to measure individual psychological factors are appropriate for evaluating behaviour change and if results from these factors provide a realistic picture of a change of behaviour and change of lifestyle, which happen in a broader and bio-psycho-social context.

Strengths

The analytical and statistical strategy of the present study is a strength, and extends existing knowledge of what is known regarding EoP in Denmark (Bredahl et al., 2008; Bredahl et al., 2010; Sorensen et al., 2006). In addition to information concerning the possible effect of various predictors, linear growth curve analysis provides information on the variability of three variance components of the individual measures obtained over an extended period of time. The richness of information increases the precision and reliability of the results and enables inference about possible factors that separately or in concert could explain the change in the outcome of interest. Furthermore, the length of the study provides long-term data not often offered in research. As the quantitative study is not a randomised trial the developments cannot be confirmed by directly comparing similar groups. But by comparing two interventions an overall estimate of best practice as the process of planning and organising the most appropriate intervention for the setting and population can be given (Driever, 2002; Green, 2001). Moreover, the analyses of development within the groups can provide valuable knowledge to researchers and practitioners of the appropriateness of the intervention as a whole, as well as specific components of the intervention (e.g., the structured intervention in the TG). It is valuable to observe development over time to understand which mechanisms in the intervention are important for behaviour change. This knowledge can be used to plan and organise more effective interventions. The results from comparisons between the groups (the TG and the PG) can provide researchers and practitioners important insight into which intervention forms possibly affect individuals in need of behaviour change towards a more physically active lifestyle.

Overall, the results of the present study indicate that factors other than the group characteristics differentiating participants in the TG and PG may explain the variability in initial levels and changes in *self-efficacy*, *stages of change* and physical activity. These finding is in accord by research showing inconsistent results of stage-based physical activity interventions (Adams & White, 2003; Sorensen et al., 2006; van Sluijs et al., 2004). Further, the present study suggests that both time-varying (e.g., lifestyle diseases, life-events, occupations and barriers) and time-invariant (e.g., family, social relations and social class) factors should be invoked in future research to disentangle the web of factors that influence the efficiency of *prescribed exercise* interventions in a community-based setting.

Qualitative results

Self-efficacy

In relation to hypothesis one, members of both groups (TG and PG) express apparently similar barriers towards becoming physically activity, and except for baseline values, their *self-efficacy* towards these barriers seems to be quite similar. In spite of this similarity of barriers and *self-efficacy*, the PG informants appeared to have a higher success rate in becoming physically active over the long-term.

Even though strong similarities between the two groups exist, they can also be distinguished from each other in one essential area. Having lifestyle diseases or bodily symptoms were described by all informants in the TG as very influential barriers, which to a great degree negatively influenced their *self-efficacy* in becoming more physically active. The same significance was not suggested by the PG informants.

> *It hurts to exercise. I get medication to ease the pain when I am exercising. That is not fun. It is really a hurdle to overcome. It gives me too many excuses for not exercising (informant TG).*

The significance of this barrier in relation to physical activity seemed to be decisive in the TG informants' behaviour changes (Biddle & Mutrie, 2007; Sallis & Hovell, 1990). It is apparent that the lifestyle diseases and bodily symptoms of the TG informants affect their *self-efficacy* in their ability to be physically active in long-term. The PG informants primarily describe moderate barriers, such as, comfort, transport and facilities. This difference between the groups could possibly provide some of the explanation as to why the PG informants seem to be successful to a greater degree in becoming physically active than do the TG informants (Sallis & Hovell, 1990). More research is needed to assess to what extent having a lifestyle disease will influence physical activity behaviour and change. Moreover, it would be relevant to investigate if specific lifestyle diseases (e.g., type 2 diabetes, hypertension, ischaemic heart disease) are more hampering for behaviour change than others. Knowledge of this would provide the possibility of differentiating the action needed to facilitate behaviour change.

Another possible explanation for the seemingly long-term difference in physical activity between the TG and the PG could be found in the results presented concerning *stages of change*. The reasons

104

the two groups give for their decision to participate in the intervention indicate that the PG informants' participation, to a greater degree than for the TG informants, is based upon interest in or motivation to participate in physical activity. The TG informants seemed to see their participation as treatment and an obligation, instead of choice or interest.

Lack of motivation and interest are indicated in research as major barriers during behaviour change or in the progression through *stages of change* (Sallis & Hovell, 1990). This is consistent with literature showing motivation or interest as an important incentive for being physically active (Biddle & Mutrie, 2007). The informants in the TG seem to use the intervention in the same way one would take prescribed medication. When the intervention stops they expect to be cured. They do not, as results indicate, use the intervention as a springboard to health development as the PG informants did, but rather as a closed package. When the intervention ends and no one else are responsible for their physical activity, they do not seem to continue doing physical activity unassisted. This may explain why most of the informants in the TG do not experience a positive progression or even experience a regression through stages over time. Findings from the interviews indicate that motivation for and an interest in the EoP intervention and physical activity are decisive in influencing the informants' *self-efficacy* towards a physically active lifestyle.

It is also possible that the intervention period is too short to have any real impact on *self-efficacy* in relation to barriers. Research shows that *self-efficacy* is a significant predictor of exercise behaviour in the early and middle stages of an exercise programme and therefore an increased effort to improve participants' *self-efficacy* in the earlier stage of the intervention is needed (McAuley et al., 1994). Furthermore, the transition from the intervention programme to unassisted training, which could be described as a key element of the intervention (Müller et al., 2007), seemed to produce new barriers in addition to those already existing. The TG informants switched from a structured programme, in which others were responsible for the organisation of the physical activity, to unassisted physical activity, for which the individual was responsible. This change in responsibility seemed to affect the TG informants' *self-efficacy* towards barriers to such a degree that adherence to physical activity failed to happen. Furthermore, informants in the TG, and also the PG, indicated a need for an increased or prolonged period of counselling from the exercise specialist. This indicates that the motivational counselling and the interventions were not effective enough or the right method to process these behaviour change issues.

In relation to hypotheses two and three and *self-efficacy* concerning barriers at baseline, both groups expressed a great deal of optimism about becoming physically active. Even though levels of *self-efficacy* seem high for members of both groups, a difference between the two were apparent. The TG informants seemed to express an increased optimism in overcoming barriers at baseline than did informants from the PG, because they were included in a structured intervention in which responsibility is placed on others, not on themselves. In spite of the TG members' seemingly higher initial *self-efficacy* towards becoming more physically active, there was no increased effect of the higher levels of baseline *self-efficacy* on the development of physical activity over the long-term.

Stages of change

In relation to hypothesis one, it seems that the PG intervention helped the informants move progressively through stages. The informants in the TG, however, had quite a dynamic process of change. For periods of the intervention, primarily right after the structured programme, the informants in the TG seemed to succeed in being physically active, but long-term adherence was not evident. Relapses to earlier *stages of change* were apparent (table 16).

In relation to hypotheses two and three, the initial levels of *stages of change* did not seem to influence compliance or adherence to physical activity in the long-term. In contrast to the hypotheses, the informants from both groups seemed to show about the same precondition and initial level with regards to levels of *stages of change*. In spite of this, the degree of physical activity over the long-term seemed to be different for the informants in the two groups. It is possible to conclude from the results, informants' statements and the illustration in table 16 (p. 99) that informants in the PG group had greater success in becoming physically active than did the informants in the treatment group. The TG informants, due to the more intense intervention, were expected to progress more positively through the stages than were the PG informants. This was predicted from previous studies of *prescribed exercise* (Kallings et al., 2008), but these findings are also supported by research showing inconsistent results of stage-based physical activity interventions promoted in primary care (Sorensen et al., 2006; van Sluijs et al., 2004). The current results suggest that preconditions of *stages of change* are not crucial for the informants' behaviour change. The findings from the interviews indicate that attitudes and intrinsic motivation towards being physically active seem to be better predictors of adherence to physical activity than are *stages of change*. Furthermore, being referred to an exercise intervention seems to produce feelings of obligation which, according to the interview data, are not conducive to behaviour change.

Social relations

The results concerning the importance of family and friends are in general in accordance with literature indicating a supportive family environment is important for achieving behaviour change (Stroebe, 2000; Trost et al., 2002). Family structure was indicated as important for adherence to physical activity. One informant articulated that being a single mother affects the possibility of maintaining behavioural change. Friends were also considered very influential, and some informants indicated that in a close-knit social pattern it could be difficult to break with long standing habits.

> *You do not change your social relations and when you try to change your behaviour they notice it. In the beginning it is cool to be different, but after a few months seeing the same people, you have returned to your old habits (informant PG).*

The interview data indicate that the GP did not influence the participants' physical activity. This is in accord with research showing that it does not matter which care provider delivers the intervention (Fleming & Godwin, 2008); but it is in contrast to research showing the GP as an important person in facilitating behaviour change in *prescribed exercise* (Camaione et al., 1997; McKenna & Vernon, 2004; Schutzer & Graves, 2004). The informants stated that the only role the GP played was to refer them to the TG or inform them about the PG. The informants received no further motivational counselling or advice from their GPs. In contrast, the exercise specialist is mentioned by a majority of the informants in both groups as an important person for facilitating behaviour change. Nevertheless, even though the informants indicated that the exercise specialist was important, it is evident that the exercise specialist did not affect *self-efficacy* concerning barriers to physical activity or influence progress through *stages of change* enough for the informants to overcome their primary barriers or adhere to a physically active lifestyle over the long-term.

With regards to the complexity of behaviour change illustrated by the bio-psycho-social model, it is not surprising that the GP is considered without influence. Seen from an interactional perspective, the traditional biomedical consultation lasting approximately 8 minutes is not comprehensive enough to encompass all relevant factors in the individual change process (Hutton & Gunn, 2007). Therefore, the role of the motivational counsellor or external care person could be emphasised in interventions like *prescribed exercise*. Since a majority of the participants argue that the exercise specialist doing the motivational counselling contributed positively to their change process and in some cases successful behaviour change, the future role of an external counsellor or care person in *prescribed exercise* interventions could be considered. Another study of *prescribed exercise* in Denmark, with an increased amount of motivational counselling from both physiotherapists and dieticians shows moderately positive results (Roessler & Ibsen, 2009). It is possible that motivational counselling used in the right way and in the right amount could have significant influence on compliance and adherence to a physically active lifestyle (Ntoumanis & Biddle, 1999). The statement below illustrates this.

> *I think the conversations have been really constructive, positive and optimistic. The basis of our conversation has been my thoughts concerning motivation and planning. She does the things I have difficulty doing like making initial contact. She has made it possible for me to get started (informant PG).*

These results are in accordance with literature showing the motivational counsellor in primary care as a key person in facilitating change (Müller et al., 2007; Steptoe et al., 2000), but also showing varied success from counselling in regards to physical activity and behaviour change (Petrella & Lattanzio, 2002). This underlines the possibility of implementing a motivational counsellor in *prescribed exercise* interventions, but also a need for research documenting which kind of counselling yields the greatest effect. Since individual psychological factors, like *stages of change* and *self-efficacy* in the motivational counselling, do not seem to be as effective as initially expected, future research on motivational counselling in *prescribed exercise* should encompass a broader and a bio-psycho-social perspective on behaviour change and lifestyle.

In *prescribed exercise*, the group training constitutes a substantial part of the intervention and therefore a potential area of influence. Within an organised exercise group, interpersonal influence can be present (or missing) in the interaction between participants, between participants and exercise specialists, but also between participants and the surrounding environment (e.g., family and friends). In the current study, the role of the other participants was expressed in two different ways. On the one hand, the other participants were often described as constituting an essential network in which the informants could feel secure because of the homogeneity of the group. The support from the group and the obligation towards the other participants were indicated as important factors to help the informants stay physically active. Following statements from participants in the TG support the fact that the group encompasses un-utilised potential in enhancing the individual's effort towards behaviour change.

If you are part of a group then you are responsible for it; that is obvious. If you start with fourteen people, you will have to be fourteen people every time, otherwise the group will shut down. You have a social obligation to be there (informant TG).

To exercise alone would not affect me the same way as exercising in a group. My expectations are for the others to be supportive and to motivate me to participate, but I do not participate for social reasons. I think it is all right to say that I do it only for me (informant TG).

To be a part of a group does not naturally lead to a successful and improved change process (Munich, 1993; Schein, 2006). Since, the participants in both interventions also express scepticism towards the other participants and experience them as limiting and intimidating, it is also relevant to discuss the possible impeding effects of the group. Examples of this could be participants not feeling a sense of connectedness with the others, a general resistance towards being part of a larger group or disliking being with other people doing physical activity.

We do not mean anything to each other. If we should try to build social relations in the group, I am not the one to contribute. I am dressed when I arrive and leave immediately after exercise. Nobody from the TG will leave lasting impressions in my mind (informant TG).

I think of them as indolent, at least it is the way I perceive them. It was the same way I perceived myself when my GP suggested the TG – an intervention for indolent people, but that is not entirely true (informant TG).

This last statement indicates a possible example of the limiting effects of the group. It could be that some participants are concerned about being categorised or stigmatised as fragile or indolent individuals because they are grouped with other people (e.g., overweight, with lifestyle diseases, inactive, and indolent lifestyles) with whom they do not desire to identify themselves.

These contradictory statements of group interaction are in accordance with research literature showing factors like cohesiveness, imparting of information and universality of suffering as important in group processes (Agazarian & Janoff, 1993; Yalom, 1985). One report recommending how to organise *prescribed exercise* in Denmark also emphasises the importance of the training group (Müller et al., 2007). This discussion of the potential of the exercise group illustrates the fact that to avoid impeding effects and to utilise the full potential of the group, the interpersonal processes within the group should be facilitated or managed to enable a positive impact for all participants. This was not the case in the TG intervention.

109

The distinction between temporary (e.g., GP, exercise specialist and other participants) and established (e.g., family and friends) social relations, evident in the different statements regarding the influence of social relations, remains an important issue. Even though the informants stated some temporary social relations were of significant importance, little or no behaviour change happened. This could indicate that even though temporary social relations hold potential, the established social relations seem to have even stronger impact on change processes than the informants indicated. This is in accordance with the literature underlining the difficulty in unfreezing, restructuring and refreezing established social relations in efforts to obtain new behaviours (Schein, 2006). Moreover, this is in accord with literature underlining behaviour as anchored in and determined by a broader context surrounding the individual and not only by individual psychological factors (Christensen & Albertsen, 2002; Johannessen, 2005; Ottesen, 1993; Thing, 2005).

Bias, imprecision and strengths

The aim of the interviews and results from the qualitative study should be considered as providing in-depth knowledge on factors of importance for individuals trying to change behaviour in *prescribed exercise* interventions. In spite of the small number of participants in the qualitative study, in-depth knowledge has been gained from individuals trying to change their behaviour. Furthermore, some comparisons between the two groups have been made and differences between the two groups indicated. Since, the design and number of participants argue for the use of an explorative approach, it is necessary to be critical when interpreting the results. Assessing differences between groups would better be answered by applying a quantitative design. Thus, it could be discussed whether the results of the study, and the differences between the two groups, are in fact related to the two different interventions or just a coincidence based on sample selection bias. Supporting this, the two groups show many similar characteristics, indicating that the results are made unclear by the small number of informants and a clearer picture could be gained from including a larger number of participants. But despite these potential biases, recurring and consistent answers within the groups in relation to the hypotheses indicate that relevant knowledge can be gained from the study, both from an explorative, but also a comparative angle, even though precautions must be taken with interpretations of the findings.

Conclusions and perspectives

"What makes sedentary people with an increased risk of lifestyle diseases change to a more physically active lifestyle?" This was the fundamental question related to behaviour change which started of the research process.

One aim was to explore to what extent behaviour change towards a more physically active lifestyle could be influenced by participating in Exercise on Prescription. A second aim was to determine if *self-efficacy* and *stages of change* would be positively influenced by participating in Exercise on Prescription. A further aim was to determine if initial levels of *self-efficacy* and *stages of change* would influence adherence to physical activity. The final aim was to explore the importance of specific social relations in regards to the participants' adherence to physical activity.

Overall, the quantitative study indicates that there was positive development in level of physical activity and *stages of change*, but no positive development in levels of *self-efficacy*. There were no differences between the Treatment Group and the Prevention Group in terms of development in levels of *self-efficacy*, *stages of change* or physical activity. Furthermore, initial levels of *self-efficacy* and *stages of change* were not decisive for adherence to level of physical activity in the long term. In summary, a *prescribed exercise* intervention including counselling and training does not enhance participants' level of *self-efficacy*, *stages of change* and physical activity compared to participants that receive counselling only. Data from the qualitative study in general are in accord with the quantitative study indicating that there were no differences in initial levels of *stages of change* between participants in the Treatment Group and the Prevention Group and that precondition in *self-efficacy* and *stages of change* is not significant for long-term development in levels of physical activity. Additionally, the quantitative study adds new and valuable information suggesting that fundamental differences between major and moderate barriers exist between the two groups. This could possibly provide some explanation for the difference (indicated in the qualitative study) between the groups in terms of adherence to long-term physical activity. Moreover, a positive attitude towards or interest in physical activity seems to be a stronger predictor of adherence to physical activity than *self-efficacy*, *stages of change* or intervention. Lastly, social relations are found to have decisive meaning for individuals trying to change behaviour.

Thus, the results do not confirm the hypotheses. This leads to considerations of what the reasons for the disappointing results could be.

1) Wrong hypotheses

One conclusion could be that the hypotheses were erroneously formulated, not encompassing results from previous research in an accurate manner. This explanation can be dismissed since leading researchers in the field of behaviour change and physical activity (e.g., Biddle, Nigg, Marshall, Mutrie, McAuley, Sallis, Marcus) have used similar hypotheses extensively and have found evidence to support them. Arguments for why the hypotheses were not confirmed must be found elsewhere.

2) Wrong Design

The way the study was designed could be a reason for the disappointing results in relation to the hypotheses. A strategy to improve the explanatory potential of future similar studies and thereby to minimise bias could be to organise the evaluation of such interventions as a double blind randomised controlled trial. A more rigid design could probably clarify possible beneficial effects of the interventions.

Even though a randomised controlled trial could have improved interpretation of the data, such a design would also be limited to providing information of a constructed "clinical" reality, thereby reducing the transferability to the complex reality in which Exercise on Prescription happens. It could be concluded that an evaluation of best practice, as performed in this study, also provides valuable knowledge – knowledge that could be used to improve the intervention and provide feedback to professionals concerning the suitability and appropriateness of the intervention. A combination of the above designs could provide valuable knowledge of not only the "clinical" issues, but also the "practical" issues of how to plan and organise an appropriate intervention for the setting and population.

3) Wrong instruments

Since the study offers no explanation as to why there were no differences found in levels of *self-efficacy*, *stages of change* and physical activity, it is important to consider the applicability and precision of the questionnaire instruments used. One cause for the disappointing results could be that the instruments used to measure levels of *self-efficacy*, *stages of change* and physical activity do not accurately reflect levels and development. In the current study, questionnaire instruments were selected from material already developed and validated in earlier research, but not validated in the target group of this study. This could possibly have introduced bias into the results. In conclusion, future studies would benefit from performing a specific validation study of the instruments. Furthermore, it could be concluded that the instruments used may not be sensitive enough to measure the medium or small changes which are expected to happen during and after EoP. If precision is not adequate, possible differences between the TG and the PG could be blurred. Moreover, it could be concluded that it is critically necessary to investigate and discuss in further detail whether measurements of *self-efficacy* and *stages of change* by questionnaire are feasible or whether other methods, such as qualitative studies, should be used.

4) No difference between the effect of the interventions
Another conclusion to explain the results could be that there really are no differences between the effect of the TG intervention and the PG intervention. If this is true, the conclusion drawn in paper III, saying that an exercise intervention supplemented by motivational counselling is not additionally effective in influencing adherence to physical activity compared to an intervention offering only motivational counselling, is correct. When designing future physical activity interventions, it should be taken into account that physical activity counselling could be just as effective (or ineffective) as physical activity combined with counselling.

5) Wrong intervention
These disappointing results entail a necessity to critically explore why offering an intense and guided training programme does not enhance adherence to physical activity in the long-term. The conclusions concerning this point are divided into three sections, which are elaborated below: a) treatment, rigidity and responsibility, b) motivational counselling and c) social relations.

a) Treatment, rigidity and responsibility
From the results and discussion, it is concluded that an area relevant for further investigation could be to determine if physical activity offered as treatment or as medicine alters the individual's perception of physical activity. If the individual perceives exercise and physical activity as a medical treatment, it is possible that they will stop exercising as soon as symptoms disappear, thereby reflecting the same pattern of non-compliance with physical activity as with ordinary prescribed medicine. It could be concluded that there should be an increased effort to avoid perceptions of physical activity as treatment and medicine.

Another explanation for the limited effect of the TG intervention compared to the PG intervention could be that a strict, structured and organised programme takes away individual initiative and responsibility, thereby pacifying and keeping the individual in the position of being treated. This perception of passivity could possibly continue with the individual after the structured part of the TG intervention has ended and maintain the conception of physical activity as the responsibility of others. It could be concluded (as apparent from the qualitative study) that physical activity is, primarily for the TG participants, perceived as an obligation rather than an enjoyable factor helping to increase quality of life. If organising physical activity in a medical setting sustains participants' conception of physical activity as treatment and the responsibility of others, it could be concluded that it is necessary to critically evaluate if physical activity could be implemented in a more appropriate way to facilitate responsibility, enjoyment and thus adherence.

b) Motivational counselling

It could be concluded, that the motivational counselling done in both the TG and the PG intervention did not, by focussing on *self-efficacy* in relation to barriers and *stages of change*, facilitate liberation from the conception of physical activity as treatment and an obligation. The counselling could better have assisted the individual in behaviour change if conversation themes had not been established in advance by the methodology of motivational interviewing and instead had focussed on individual issues of importance in regarding physical activity as a possibility of enjoyment and enhanced quality of life.

c) Social relations

Another conclusion is that social relations play a much larger part in influencing behaviour change than initially assumed. It could be concluded that an external care person (the motivational counsellor, the exercise specialist or the GP) holds potential for playing an important role in future *prescribed exercise* interventions. However, the type, amount and duration of the counselling need to be explored to a greater extent. Other social relations during the intervention, such as family, friends and training group were also shown as important potential areas of influence. It could also be concluded that the training or exercise group yields great potential in influencing the change process and adherence of the individual. If the potential of group processes and interactions between individuals are facilitated in a scientifically substantiated way, this could contribute to a successful change process towards a physically active lifestyle. Future research should investigate this. It could also be concluded that the attitude of family and friends towards changes of lifestyle could be a potential area of significant influence on physical activity behaviour. Thus, attitudes of family and friends may affect adherence to a physically active lifestyle to a greater degree than initially assumed. Further research is needed to establish this connection.

Perspectives

From the above conclusions, it could be summarised that wrong design, wrong instruments or wrong intervention could offer some explanations for the disappointing results in relation to the hypotheses. But when these conclusions are related to the bio-psycho-social model and health psychology, it could be stated that determinants other than individual psychological factors, design and intervention may be more important for behaviour change and may possibly explain why the hypotheses are not supported here.

Physical activity behaviour has to be considered in context and it has to be recognised that health behaviour is not only determined by specific individual psychological and social factors but influenced by conditions of life, way of life and lifestyle in general. This leads to a necessity for a broadened perspective on physical activity interventions like Exercise on Prescription. From the relation between conditions of life, way of life, lifestyle and health behaviour, it could be concluded that since Exercise on Prescription only focuses on and influences physical activity behaviour, it does not adequately or sufficiently influence the overall individual's lifestyle, but just a limited part of it. Even though the participants may wish for behaviour change and enhanced physical activity, other areas in the individuals' bio-psycho-social context may impact behaviour to a greater extent and thereby inhibit change over the long-term. Exercise on Prescription may have the weight to influence physical activity behaviour temporarily, but it is far from certain that such an influence holds the potential to affect the individual lifestyle and moreover impact the individual disease in the long-term, due to its coherence with a bio-psycho-social context. Even though a multi-disciplinary analysis, as conducted by the adjusted Health Technology Assessment of Exercise on Prescription in Denmark (the current study representing the patient perspective), presents knowledge of EoP in four essential areas included in the bio-psycho-social model, it could be concluded that this knowledge is not ample enough to encompass and describe the interactions between individual health behaviour, lifestyle, way of life and conditions of life. Acknowledging this, future research with a basis in a bio-psycho-social approach should acknowledge the interactional basis of behavioural change and to a greater degree attempt to take into account the interaction between the individual and areas such as social class, family, friends, social relations, general practitioner, exercise specialist, and the training group and consider their influence on the individual's lifestyle, coping, health behaviour and reactions to illness and disease. Thus, because this thesis does not, future research concerning Exercise on Prescription, behaviour change and physical activity should make an effort to include the above-mentioned interactional factors in the analysis of behaviour change. A systemic, holistic or ecological analysis of individuals trying to change behaviour could possibly provide a better analytical basis, adding essential knowledge and thereby enhancing researchers' and practitioners' possibilities for improving the concept Exercise on Prescription.

Future research

When relating the results, discussions and conclusions of this thesis towards future research, the acknowledgments of this thesis have confirmed that focussing on individual factors is not enough and that a bio-psycho-social and integrative perspective is necessary for understanding behaviour and behaviour change. Even though the results from the thesis were disappointing in relation to the hypotheses, they have also generated new and interesting acknowledgements which can shed light on inspiring and motivating topics for future research. It is still motivating and relevant to explore which factors enhance motivation for life-long physical activity. But instead of focussing on individual factors such as *self-efficacy* and *stages of change*, other factors could be more important for behaviour change. Such factors, e.g., could be the significance of family and friends, exercise instructors, motivational counsellors and the significance of the dynamics in a training group. Furthermore, other factors, like the participants' conception of physical activity as treatment and the structure of interventions inducing irresponsibility or responsibility of participants, would also be relevant areas for further research.

Most of all, it has to be realised that motivation and inclination to exercise are especially important. It has to be recognised that participation in physical activity interventions does not automatically induce motivation and inclination for physical activity. It is not possible to counsel, converse or intervene yourselves or others to the life-long integration of physical activity, without fundamental motivation and conceptions of physical activity as enjoyable, motivating and rewarding. One way to engender a life-long motivation for exercise and physical activity could be to develop a model for understanding participation in exercise and physical activity that shifts the emphasis away from a focus on treatment, health and behaviour change and towards motivation, meaning and enjoyment. This approach could be relevant for discussing new ways of thinking when working to improve public health policy and practice, with the intention of encouraging life-long participation in exercise in general. A reconceptualising of participation in physical activity in this way could help answer the question: "What makes sedentary people with an increased risk of lifestyle diseases change to a more physically active lifestyle?", and thereby enhance adherence to physical activity and moreover possibly influence those in greatest need.

References

1   Aadahl M. & Jorgensen T. Validation of a new self-report instrument for measuring physical activity. *Med Sci Sports Exerc*. 2003: 35(7): 1196-1202.

2   ACSM. American College of Sports Medicine Position Stand. The recommended quantity and quality of exercise for developing and maintaining cardiorespiratory and muscular fitness, and flexibility in healthy adults. *Med Sci Sports Exerc*. 1998: 30(6): 975-991.

3   Adams J. & White M. Are activity promotion interventions based on the transtheoretical model effective? A critical review. *Br J Sports Med*. 2003: 37(2): 106-114.

4   Adams J. & White M. Why don't stage-based activity promotion interventions work? *Health Educ Res*. 2005: 20(2): 237-243.

5   Adams S.A., Matthews C.E., Ebbeling C.B., Moore C.G., Cunningham J.E., Fulton J. and Hebert J.R. The effect of social desirability and social approval on self-reports of physical activity. *American Journal of Epidemiology*. 2005: 161(4): 389-398.

6   Ader R. & Cohen N. Psychoneuroimmunology: conditioning and stress. *Annu Rev Psychol*. 1993: 44: 53-85.

7   Agazarian, Y. M. and Janoff, S. (1993). Systems Theory and Small Groups. In Kaplan, H. I. and Sadock, B. J., *Comprehensive group psychotherapy* (3. edition ed., 32-44). Baltimore, Md.: Williams & Wilkins.

8   Agger, N. P. (1991). *Psykologisk behandling ved somatisk sygdom*. Kbh.: Komiteen for Sundhedsoplysning.

9   Ainslie P., Reilly T. and Westerterp K. Estimating human energy expenditure: a review of techniques with particular reference to doubly labelled water. *Sports Med*. 2003: 33(9): 683-698.

10 Ainsworth B.E., Haskell W.L., Whitt M.C., Irwin M.L., Swartz A.M., Strath S.J., O'Brien W.L., Bassett D.R., Jr., Schmitz K.H., Emplaincourt P.O., Jacobs D.R., Jr. and Leon A.S. Compendium of physical activities: an update of activity codes and MET intensities. *Med Sci Sports Exerc*. 2000: 32(9 Suppl): S498-S504.

11 Ainsworth B.E., Jacobs D.R., Jr. and Leon A.S. Validity and reliability of self-reported physical activity status: the Lipid Research Clinics questionnaire. *Med Sci Sports Exerc*. 1993a: 25(1): 92-98.

12 Ainsworth B.E., Leon A.S., Richardson M.T., Jacobs D.R. and Paffenbarger R.S., Jr. Accuracy of the College Alumnus Physical Activity Questionnaire. *J Clin Epidemiol*. 1993b: 46(12): 1403-1411.

13 Aittasalo M., Miilunpalo S., Kukkonen-Harjula K. and Pasanen M. A randomized intervention of physical activity promotion and patient self-monitoring in primary health care. *Prev Med.* 2006: 42(1): 40-46.

14 Ajzen I. The theory of planned behavior. *Organizational Behavior and Human Decision Processes.* 1991: 50: 179-211.

15 Ajzen, I. and Fishbein, M. (1980). *Understanding attitudes and predicting social behavior.* New Jersey: Prentice-Hall, Inc., Englewood Cliffs.

16 Almind, G. and Hansen, G. R. (2009). Forebyggelse og analyse på individniveau. In Kamper-Jørgensen, F, Almind, G., and Jensen, B. B., *Forebyggende sundhedsarbejde: baggrund, analyse og teori, arbejdsmetoder* (5. udgave ed., 173-180). Kbh.: Munksgaard Danmark.

17 Altman, D. G. (1999). *Practical Statistics for Medical Research.* London: Chapman & Hall/CRC.

18 Andersen, H. (1998). *Sociologi - en grundbog til et fag.* København: Hans Reitzels Forlag A/S.

19 Andersen L.B., Schnohr P., Schroll M. and Hein H.O. All-cause mortality associated with physical activity during leisure time, work, sports, and cycling to work. *Arch Intern Med.* 2000: 160(11): 1621-1628.

20 Andreassen, P. (2007). *Evaluering af Region Syddanmarks projekt Motion som Medicin - Organisering og motionsformidling.* Region Syddanmark.

21 Antonovsky, A. (1979). *Health, Stress and Coping: New perspectives on mental and physical Well-Being.* San Francisco: Jossey-Bass.

22 Antonovsky, A. (2000). *Helbredets mysterium.* København: Hans Reitzels Forlag A/S.

23 Balint G.P., Buchanan W.W. and Dequeker J. A brief history of medical taxonomy and diagnosis. *Clinical Rheumatology.* 2006: 25(2): 132-135.

24 Bandura, A. (1986). *Social foundations of thought and action: A social cognitive theory.* Englewood Cliffs, N.J: Prentice-Hall.

25 Bandura, A. (1995). *Self-efficacy In Changing Societies.* Cambridge University Press.

26 Bandura, A. (1997). *Self-efficacy, The Exercise of Control.* New York: W.H. Freeman and Company.

27 Barkham M. & Mellor-Clark J. Bridging evidence-based practice and practice-based evidence: developing a rigorous and relevant knowledge for the psychological therapies. *Clinical Psychology & Psychotherapy.* John Wiley & Sons, Ltd. 2003: 10(6): 319-327.

28 Beaton D.E., Bombardier C., Guillemin F. and Ferraz M.B. Guidelines for the process of cross-cultural adaptation of self-report measures. *Spine.* 2000: 25(24): 3186-3191.

29 Benini A. & Deleo J.A. Rene Descartes' physiology of pain. *Spine.* 1999: 24(20): 2115-2119.

30 Benisovich S.V., Rossi J.S., Norman G.J. and Nigg C.R. Development of a multidimensional measure of exercise self-efficacy. New Orleans, LA: *Society of Behavioral Medicine (SBM)*. 1998.

31 Bennett J.W. & Chung K.T. Alexander Fleming and the discovery of penicillin. *Advances in Applied Microbiology*. San Diego: Academic Press Inc. 2001:(49): 163-184.

32 Bess H. Self-efficacy and the Stages of Exercise Behavior Change. *Research Quarterly for Exercise and sport*. Academic Research Library. 1992: 63(1): 60-66.

33 Biddle S.J. & Fox K.R. Motivation for physical activity and weight management. *Int J Obes Relat Metab Disord*. 1998: 22 Suppl 2: 39-47.

34 Biddle, S. J., Hagger, M. S., Chatzisarantis, N. L., and Lippke, S. (2007). Theoretical Frameworks in Exercise Psychology. In Tenenbaum, G. and Eklund, R. C., *Handbook of Sport Psychology* (3 ed., 537-559). New Jersey: John Wiley & Sons, Inc.

35 Biddle, S. J. and Mutrie, N. (2007). *Psychology of Physical Activity. Determinants, well-being and interventions*. (2 ed.) London: Routledge.

36 Biddle S.J.H. & Nigg C.R. Theories of exercise behavior. *International Journal of Sport Psychology*. 2000: 31(2): 290-304.

37 Blair S.N., Kampert J.B., Kohl H.W., III, Barlow C.E., Macera C.A., Paffenbarger R.S., Jr. and Gibbons L.W. Influences of cardiorespiratory fitness and other precursors on cardiovascular disease and all-cause mortality in men and women. *JAMA*. 1996: 276(3): 205-210.

38 Bolman C. & De Vries H. Psycho-social determinants and motivational phases in smoking behavior of cardiac inpatients. *Prev Med*. 1998: 27(5 Pt 1): 738-747.

39 Booth M. Assessment of physical activity: an international perspective. *Res Q Exerc Sport*. 2000: 71(2 Suppl): S114-S120.

40 Booth M.L., Macaskill P., Owen N., Oldenburg B., Marcus B.H. and Bauman A. Population prevalence and correlates of stages of change in physical activity. *Health Educ Q*. 1993: 20(3): 431-440.

41 Booth M.L., Okely A.D., Chey T.N. and Bauman A. The reliability and validity of the Adolescent Physical Activity Recall Questionnaire. *Med Sci Sports Exerc*. 2002: 34(12): 1986-1995.

42 Bredahl T.V., Puggaard L. and Roessler K.K. Exercise on Prescription. Effect of attendance on participants' psychological factors in a Danish version of Exercise on Prescription, A Study Protocol. *BMC Health Serv Res*. 2008: 8(1): 139

43 Bredahl, T. V. G., Gårn, A., Kristensen, T., Puggaard, L., Skovgaard, T., Sørensen, J., Sørensen, J. B., and Aagaard, P. G. (2010). *Resultatopsamling af Motion På Recept i Danmark*. København: Sundhedsstyrelsen.

44 Brown T.M. & Fee E. Rudolf Carl Virchow: medical scientist, social reformer, role model. *Am J Public Health*. 2006: 96(12): 2104-2105.

45 Camaione D.N., Burns K.J. and Chatterton C.T. Counseling for physical activity: what primary-care physicians should know. *Conn Med*. 1997: 61(7): 391-395.

46 Cardinal B.J. & Kosma M. Self-efficacy and the stages and processes of change associated with adopting and maintaining muscular fitness-promoting behaviors. *Res Q Exerc Sport*. 2004: 75(2): 186-196.

47 Caspersen C.J., Powell K.E. and Christenson G.M. Physical activity, exercise, and physical fitness: definitions and distinctions for health-related research. *Public Health Rep*. 1985: 100(2): 126-131.

48 Chatzisarantis, N. L. D. and Hagger, M. S. (2007). Intrinsic Motivation and Self-determination in Exercise and Sport. Reflecting on the Past and Sketching the Future. In Hagger, M. S. and Chatzisarantis, N. L. D., *Intrinsic Motivation and Self-determination in Exercise and Sport* (281-296). Champaign, IL: Human Kinetics.

49 Christensen, U. and Albertsen, K. (2002). Teorier om dannelse og forandring af livsstil. In Iversen, L., Kristensen, T. K., Holstein, B. E., and Due, P., *Medicinsk Sociologi. Samfund, Sundhed og Sygdom* (1 ed., 207-224). København: Munksgaard.

50 Christensen, V. (1988). Sundhed for alle. In Nellemann, G, *Dagligliv i Danmark i vor tid 1* (247-273). København: Nyt Nordisk Forlag, Arnold Busck.

51 Christensen, V. and Sommer, B. (2002). *Socialmedicinsk grundbog: fra offer til aktør*. (3. udgave ed.) Kbh.: Munksgaard Danmark.

52 Cohen S., Doyle W.J., Skoner D.P., Rabin B.S. and Gwaltney J.M., Jr. Social ties and susceptibility to the common cold. *JAMA*. 1997: 277(24): 1940-1944.

53 Conway J.M., Irwin M.L. and Ainsworth B.E. Estimating energy expenditure from the Minnesota Leisure Time Physical Activity and Tecumseh Occupational Activity questionnaires - a doubly labeled water validation. *J Clin Epidemiol*. 2002a: 55(4): 392-399.

54 Conway J.M., Seale J.L, Jacobs D.R., Jr., Irwin M.L. and Ainsworth B.E. Comparison of energy expenditure estimates from doubly labeled water, a physical activity questionnaire, and physical activity records. *Am J Clin Nutr*. 2002b: 75(3): 519-525.

55 Craig C.L., Marshall A.L., Sjostrom M., Bauman A.E., Booth M.L., Ainsworth B.E., Pratt M., Ekelund U., Yngve A., Sallis J.F. and Oja P. International physical activity questionnaire: 12-country reliability and validity. *Med Sci Sports Exerc*. 2003: 35(8): 1381-1395.

56 Dahler-Larsen, P. (2005). *At fremstille kvalitative data*. (3 ed.) Odense: Syddansk Universitetsforlag.

57 Dannecker E.A., Hausenblas H.A., Connaughton D.P. and Lovins T.R. Validation of a stages of exercise change questionnaire. *Res Q Exerc Sport*. 2003: 74(3): 236-247.

58   De Vries H. Self-efficacy: The third factor besides attitue and subjektive norm as a predictor of behavioral intensions. *Health Education Research*. 1988: 3: 273-282.

59   De Vries H. Predicting stage transitions for smoking cessation applying the attitude-social influence-efficacy model. *Psychology and Health*. 1998: 13: 369-385.

60   De Vries H., Mudde A.N., Dijkstra A. and Willemsen M.C. Differential beliefs, perceived social influences, and self-efficacy expectations among smokers in various motivational phases. *Prev Med*. 1998: 27(5 Pt 1): 681-689.

61   Deci, E. L. and Ryan, R. M. (1991). A Motivational Approach to Self: Integration in Personality. In Dienstbier, R., *Nebraska symposium on motivation: Perspectives on motivation* (38 ed., 237-288). Lincoln, NE: University of Nebraska Press.

62   Denzin, N. and Lincoln, Y. (2005). *The SAGE handbook of qualitative research*. (3 ed.) Thousand Oaks, California: Sage Publications.

63   Dewalt D.A. & Pincus T. The legacies of Rudolf Virchow: Cellular medicine in the 20th century and social medicine in the 21st century. *Israel Medical Association Journal*. 2003: 5(6): 395-397.

64   Driever M.J. Are evidenced-based practice and best practice the same? *West J Nurs Res*. 2002: 24(5): 591-597.

65   Due, P. and Holstein, B. (2009). Sundhedsadfærd. In Kamper-Jørgensen, F, Almind, G., and Jensen, B. B., *Forebyggende sundhedsarbejde: baggrund, analyse og teori, arbejdsmetoder* (5. udgave ed., 209-219). Kbh.: Munksgaard Danmark.

66   Dugdill L., Graham R.C. and McNair F. Exercise referral: the public health panacea for physical activity promotion? A critical perspective of exercise referral schemes; their development and evaluation. *Ergonomics*. 2005: 48(11-14): 1390-1410.

67   Edlund W., Gronseth G., So Y. and Franklin G. Clinical Practice Guideline Process Manual. American Academy of of Neurology. St. Paul, M.N.: *American Academy of Neurology*. 2004.

68   Edmunds J., Ntoumanis N. and Duda J.L. Adherence and well-being in overweight and obese patients referred to an exercise on prescription scheme: A self-determination theory perspective. *Psychology of Sport and Exercise*. 2008: 8: 722-740.

69   Eichberg, H. (1993). Livsstil som indikator. Modernisering eller revolution i bevægelseskulturen. In Riiskjær, S., *Krop og livsstil* (16-46). Slagelse: Bavnebanke.

70   Elley C.R., Kerse N., Arroll B. and Robinson E. Effectiveness of counselling patients on physical activity in general practice: cluster randomised controlled trial. *BMJ*. 2003: 326(7393): 793.

71   Elsass, P. (2000). *Sundhedspsykologi, et nyt fag mellem humaniora og naturvidenskab*. Haslev: Gyldendal.

72   Elsass, P., Friis-Hasché, E., and Nielsen, T. (2004). *Klinisk sundhedspsykologi*. (1. udgave ed.) Kbh.: Munksgaard Danmark.

73 Elsass, P. and Lauritsen, P. (2006). *Humanistisk sundhedsforskning: teori, metode, praksis*. (1. udgave ed.) Kbh.: Hans Reitzel.

74 Engel G. The Need for a New Medical Model: A Challenge for Biomedicine. *Science*. 1977: 196(4282): 129-136.

75 Engel G. Sounding Board, The Biopsychosocial Model and Medical Education. *The New England Journal of Medicine*. 1982: 306(13): 802-805.

76 Engel G.L. How Much Longer Must Medicines Science be Bound by A 17Th-Century World-View (Reprinted from the Task of Medicine, Pg 113-136, 1988). *Psychotherapy and Psychosomatics*. 1992: 57(1-2): 3-16.

77 Engel G.L. From biomedical to biopsychosocial .1. Being scientific in the human domain. *Psychotherapy and Psychosomatics*. 1997: 66(2): 57-62.

78 Engelhardt, D. (2001). *Paracelsus im Urteil der Naturwissenschaften und Medizin des 18. und 19. Jahrhunderts: Darstellung, Quellen, Forschungsliteratur*. Heidelberg: Barth.

79 Fenton M. Battling America's epidemic of physical inactivity: building more walkable, livable communities. *J Nutr Educ Behav*. 2005: 37 Suppl 2: S115-S120.

80 Fleming P. & Godwin M. Lifestyle interventions in primary care: systematic review of randomized controlled trials. *Can Fam Physician*. 2008: 54(12): 1706-1713.

81 Flemming A. Classics In Infectious Diseases. On the Antibacterial Action of Cultures of a Penicillum, with Special Reference to Their Use in the Isolation of B. Influenzae. *Reviews Of Infectious Diseases*. 1980: 2(1): 129-139.

82 Fox K., Biddle S., Edmunds L., Bowler I. and Killoran A. Physical activity promotion through primary health care in England. *Br J Gen Pract*. 1997: 47(419): 367-369.

83 Fox, M., Green, G., and Martin, P. (2007). *Doing practitioner research*. London: SAGE.

84 Goldsworthy P.D. & McFarlane A.C. Howard Florey, Alexander Fleming and the fairy tale of penicillin. *Med J Aust*. 2002: 176(4): 176-178.

85 Green L.W. From research to "best practices" in other settings and populations. *Am J Health Behav*. 2001: 25(3): 165-178.

86 Gubrium, J. F. and Holstein, J. A. (2001). *Handbook of interview research: context and method*. London: Sage Publications.

87 Hagger M.S., Biddle S. and Chatzisarantis N. A Meta-Analytic Review of the Theories of Resoned Action and Planned Behavior in Physical Activity: Predictive Validity and the Constribution of Additional Variables. *Journal of Sport & Exercise Psychology*. Human Kinetics Publishers, Inc. 2002: 24: 3-32.

88 Hagger, M. S. and Chatzisarantis, N. L. D. (2007). *Intrinsic motivation and self-determination in exercise and sport*. Champaign, IL: Human Kinetics.

89 Harada N.D., Chiu V., King A.C. and Stewart A.L. An evaluation of three self-report physical activity instruments for older adults. *Med Sci Sports Exerc.* 2001: 33(6): 962-970.

90 Harland J., White M., Drinkwater C., Chinn D., Farr L. and Howel D. The Newcastle exercise project: a randomised controlled trial of methods to promote physical activity in primary care. *BMJ.* 1999: 319(7213): 828-832.

91 Harrison R.A., McNair F. and Dugdill L. Access to exercise referral schemes - a population based analysis. *J Public Health (Oxf).* 2005a: 27(4): 326-330.

92 Harrison R.A., Roberts C. and Elton P.J. Does primary care referral to an exercise programme increase physical activity one year later? A randomized controlled trial. *J Public Health (Oxf).* 2005b: 27(1): 25-32.

93 Haskell W.L., Lee I.M., Pate R.R., Powell K.E., Blair S.N., Franklin B.A., Macera C.A., Heath G.W., Thompson P.D. and Bauman A. Physical activity and public health: updated recommendation for adults from the American College of Sports Medicine and the American Heart Association. *Circulation.* 2007: 116(9): 1081-1093.

94 Hea, R. (2008). *Sundhedsprofiler i Region Syddanmarks Motion på Recept. Resultater* Vejle, Danmark: Region Syddanmark.

95 Hellerstein D.J. Practice-based evidence rather than evidence-based practice in psychiatry. *Medscape J Med.* 2008: 10(6): 141.

96 Hellsten L.A., Nigg C., Norman G., Burbank P., Braun L., Breger R., Coday M., Elliot D., Garber C., Greaney M., Lees F., Matthews C., Moe E., Resnick B., Riebe D., Rossi J., Toobert D. and Wang T. Accumulation of behavioral validation evidence for physical activity stage of change. *Health Psychol.* 2008: 27(1 Suppl): S43-S53.

97 Hillsdon, M., Foster, C., Cavill, N., Crombie, H., and Naidoo, B. (2005). *The effectiveness of public health interventions for increasing physical activity among adults: a review of reviews* London: Health Development Agency.

98 Holm K., Kremers S.P. and de Vries H. Why do Danish adolescents take up smoking? *Eur J Public Health.* 2003: 13(1): 67-74.

99 Hutton C.M. & Gunn J. Do longer consultations improve the management of psychological problems in general practice? A systematic literature review. *BMC Health Serv Res.* 2007: 7(1): 71.

100 Iversen, L. (2002). *Medicinsk sociologi. Samfund, sundhed og sygdom.* København: Munksgaard.

101 Jackson C., Smith R.A. and Conner M. Applying an extended version of the theory of planned behaviour to physical activity. *J Sports Sci.* 2003: 21(2): 119-133.

102 Jacobs D.R., Ainsworth B.E., Hartman T.J. and Leon A.S. A simultaneous evaluation of 10 commonly used physical activity questionnaires. *Med Sci Sports Exerc.* 1993: 25(1): 81-91.

103 Jensen, B. B. (2009). Sundhedspædagogiske kernebegreber. In Kamper-Jørgensen, F, Almind, G., and Jensen, B. B., *Forebyggende sundhedsarbejde: baggrund, analyse og teori, arbejdsmetoder* (5. udgave ed., 220-238). Kbh.: Munksgaard Danmark.

104 Johannessen, H. (2005). *Pædagoger og sundhedsarbejde: en bog om levekår, livsstil og helbred.* (2. udgave ed.) Kbh.: Munksgaard Danmark.

105 Jones F., Harris P., Waller H. and Coggins A. Adherence to an exercise prescription scheme: the role of expectations, self-efficacy, stage of change and psychological well-being. *Br J Health Psychol.* 2005: 10(Pt 3): 359-378.

106 Jorgensen T., Hvenegaard A. and Kristensen F.B. Health technology assessment in Denmark. *Int J Technol Assess Health Care.* 2000: 16(2): 347-381.

107 Kallings L.V., Leijon M., Hellenius M.L. and Stahle A. Physical activity on prescription in primary health care: a follow-up of physical activity level and quality of life. *Scand J Med Sci Sports.* 2008: 18(2): 154-161.

108 Kirkwood, B. and Sterne, J. (2003). *Essential medical statistics.* (2 ed.) Malden, Massachussets: Blackwell Science.

109 Kleinman, A. (1988). *The Illness Narratives. Suffering, Healing & The Human Condition.* (1 ed.) United States of America: Basic Books.

110 Kristensen, F. B. and Sigmund, H. (2007). *Metodehåndbog for Medicinsk Teknologivurdering* København: Sundhedsstyrelsen, Enhed for Medicinsk Teknologivurdering.

111 Kvale, S. (2003). *En introduktion til det kvalitative forskningsinterview.* (9 ed.) København: Hans Reitzels Forlag.

112 Lakerveld J., Ijzelenber W., van Tulder M.W., Hellemans I.M., Rauwerda J.A., van Rossum A.C. and Seidell J.C. Motives for (not) participating in a lifestyle intervention trial. *BMC Med Res Methodol.* 2008: 8(1): 17.

113 Lazarus, R. and Folkman, S. (1984). *Stress, Appraisal and Coping.* New York: Springer Publishing Company.

114 Lindstrom J., Ilanne-Parikka P., Peltonen M., Aunola S., Eriksson JG., Hemio K., Hamalainen H., Harkonen P., Keinanen-Kiukaanniemi S., Laakso M., Louheranta A., Mannelin M., Paturi M., Sundvall J., Valle T.T., Uusitupa M. and Tuomilehto J. Sustained reduction in the incidence of type 2 diabetes by lifestyle intervention: follow-up of the Finnish Diabetes Prevention Study. *Lancet.* 2006: 368(9548): 1673-1679.

115 Lund, R. and Due, P. (2002). Sociale relationer og helbred. In Iversen, L., Kristensen, T. S., Holstein, B., and Due, P., *Medicinsk sociologi. Samfund, sundhed og sygdom.* (87-104). København: Munksgaard.

116 Lutgendorf S.K. & Costanzo E.S. Psychoneuroimmunology and health psychology: An integrative model. *Brain Behavior and Immunity.* 2003: 17(4): 225-232.

117 Marcus B.H., Banspach S.W., Lefebvre R.C., Rossi J.S., Carleton R.A. and Abrams D.B.
Using the stages of change model to increase the adoption of physical activity among
community participants. *Am J Health Promot.* 1992a: 6(6): 424-429.

118 Marcus B.H., Selby V.C., Niaura R.S. and Rossi J.S. Self-efficacy and the stages of exercise
behavior change. *Res Q Exerc Sport.* 1992b: 63(1): 60-66.

119 Marcus B.H. & Simkin L.R. The transtheoretical model: applications to exercise behavior.
Med Sci Sports Exerc. 1994: 26(11): 1400-1404.

120 Marshall S.J. & Biddle S.J. The transtheoretical model of behavior change: a meta-analysis of
applications to physical activity and exercise. *Ann Behav Med.* 2001: 23(4): 229-246.

121 Marx O.M. What is the history of psychiatry? *Hist Psychiatry.* 1992: 3(11): 279-301.

122 McAuley E. Self-efficacy and the maintenance of exercise participation in older adults. *J
Behav Med.* 1993: 16(1): 103-113.

123 McAuley E. & Blissmer B. Self-efficacy determinants and consequences of physical activity.
Exerc Sport Sci Rev. 2000: 28(2): 85-88.

124 McAuley E., Courneya K.S., Rudolph D.L. and Lox C.L. Enhancing exercise adherence in
middle-aged males and females. *Prev Med.* 1994: 23(4): 498-506.

125 McAuley E., Jerome G.J., Elavsky S., Marquez D.X. and Ramsey S.N. Predicting long-term
maintenance of physical activity in older adults. *Prev Med.* 2003: 37(2): 110-118.

126 McKenna J. & Vernon M. How general practitioners promote 'lifestyle' physical activity.
Patient Educ Couns. 2004: 54(1): 101-106.

127 McKnight, P. E., McKnight, K. M., Sidani, S., and Figueredo, A. J. (2007). *Missing data: a
gentle introduction.* New York, NY: Guilford Press.

128 Miller, W. R. and Rollnick, S. (2002). *Motivational interviewing: preparing people for
change.* (2 ed.) New York: The Guilford Press.

129 Milner, J. (1996). *Politikens store fremmedordbog.* Haslev: Politikens Forlag A/S.

130 Modeste, N. N. (1996). *Dictionary of Public Health Promotion and Education. Terms and
Concepts.* Thousand Oaks, California: SAGE Publications, Inc.

131 Motl R.W., McAuley E. and DiStefano C. Is social desirability associated with self-reported
physical activity? *Preventive Medicine.* 2005: 40(6): 735-739.

132 Müller, H., Gårn, A., and Holt, A. (2007). *Motion på Recept - erfaringer og anbefalinger*
Sund By Netværket.

133 Munich, R. L. (1993). Group Dynamics. In Kaplan, H. I. and Sadock, B. J., *Comprehensive
group psychotherapy* (3. edition ed., 21-32). Baltimore, Md.: Williams & Wilkins.

134 Nigg, C. R. (2002). Physical Activity Assessment Issues in Population Based Interventions: A Stage Approach. In Welk, G. J., *Physical Activity Assessments for Health-Related Research* (227-239). Human Kinetics.

135 Nigg C.R. There is more to stages of exercise than just exercise. *Exerc Sport Sci Rev*. 2005: 33(1): 32-35.

136 Nigg C.R., Norman G.J., Rossi J.S. and Benisovich S.V. Processes of exercise behavior change: Redeveloping the scale. San Diego, CA: *Society of Behavioral Medicine (SBM)*. 1999.

137 Nigg, C. R., Rossi, J. S., Norman, G. J., and Benisovich, S. V. (1998). Structure of decisional balance for exercise adoption. In *19th annual meeting of the Society of Behavioral Medicine*. Conference Proceeding.

138 Norman A., Bellocco R., Bergstrom A. and Wolk A. Validity and reproducibility of self-reported total physical activity - differences by relative weight. *Int J Obes Relat Metab Disord*. 2001: 25(5): 682-688.

139 Norman, G. J., Benisovich, S. V., Nigg, C. R., and Rossi, J. S. (1998). Examining three exercise staging algorithms in two samples. In *19th annual meeting of the Society of Behavioral Medicine*.

140 Ntoumanis N. & Biddle S.J. A review of motivational climate in physical activity. *J Sports Sci*. 1999: 17(8): 643-665.

141 O' Sullivan I., Orbell S., Rakow T. and Parker R. Prospective research in health service settings: Health psychology, science and the 'Hawthorne' effect. *Journal of Health Psychology*. 2004: 9(3): 355-359.

142 Olsen, H. (2002). *Kvalitative Kvaler. Kvalitative metoder og danske kvalitative interviewundersøgelsers kvalitet*. København: Akademisk Forlag A/S.

143 Ottesen, L. (1993). Idræt og livsformer. Om forholdet mellem levevilkår, livsformer og livsstil. In Riiskjær, S., *Krop og livsstil* (47-57). Slagelse: Bavnebanke.

144 Paffenbarger R.S., Blair S.N., Lee I.M. and Hyde R.T. Measurement of physical activity to assess health effects in free-living populations. *Med Sci Sports Exerc*. 1993: 25(1): 60-70.

145 Paweletz N. Birth of the life sciences in The Netherlands and Belgium. *Nat Rev Mol Cell Biol*. 2001: 2(11): 857-863.

146 Pedersen, B. (2005). *Motion på recept: motion som behandling*. (Særudgave ed.) København: Nyt Nordisk Forlag.

147 Pedersen, B. K. (2003). *Recept på motion. Motion som forebyggelse*. Nyt Nordisk Forlag Arnold Busck A/S.

148 Pedersen B.K. & Saltin B. Evidence for prescribing exercise as therapy in chronic disease. *Scand J Med Sci Sports*. 2006: 16 Suppl 1: 3-63.

149 Petrella R.J. & Lattanzio C.N. Does counseling help patients get active? Systematic review of the literature. *Can Fam Physician.* 2002: 48: 72-80.

150 Philippaerts R.M., Westerterp K.R. and Lefevre J. Doubly labelled water validation of three physical activity questionnaires. *Int J Sports Med.* 1999: 20(5): 284-289.

151 Philippaerts R.M., Westerterp K.R. and Lefevre J. Comparison of two questionnaires with a tri-axial accelerometer to assess physical activity patterns. *Int J Sports Med.* 2001: 22(1): 34-39.

152 Prochaska J.O. & Diclemente C.C. Stages and processes of self-change of smoking: toward an integrative model of change. *J Consult Clin Psychol.* 1983: 51(3): 390-395.

153 Prochaska J.O. & Velicer W.F. The transtheoretical model of health behavior change. *Am J Health Promot.* 1997: 12(1): 38-48.

154 Rabe-Hesketh, S. and Skrondal, A. (2008). *Multilevel and Longitudinal Modeling Using Stata.* (2 ed.) College Station, Texas: StataCorp LP.

155 Rabin, B. S. (1999). *Stress, immune function, and health: The connection.* New York: Wiley-Liss.

156 Rabin B.S., Cohen S., Ganguli R., Lysle D.T. and Cunnick J.E. Bidirectional interaction between the central nervous system and the immune system. *Crit Rev Immunol.* 1989: 9(4): 279-312.

157 Ramian K. Evidens på egne præmisser. *Psykolog Nyt.* København: Dansk Psykolog Forening. 2009:(2): 18-25.

158 Reed G.R., Velicer W.F., Prochaska J.O., Rossi J.S. and Marcus B.H. What makes a good staging algorithm: examples from regular exercise. *Am J Health Promot.* 1997: 12(1): 57-66.

159 Regeringen (2002). *Sund hele livet - de nationale mål og strategier for folkesundheden 2002-10.* København: Indenrigs- og Sundhedsministeriet.

160 Rennie K.L. & Wareham N.J. The validation of physical activity instruments for measuring energy expenditure: problems and pitfalls. *Public Health Nutr.* 1998: 1(4): 265-271.

161 Richardson M.T., Leon A.S., Jacobs D.R., Jr., Ainsworth B.E. and Serfass R. Comprehensive evaluation of the Minnesota Leisure Time Physical Activity Questionnaire. *J Clin Epidemiol.* 1994: 47(3): 271-281.

162 Riebe D., Garber C.E., Rossi J.S., Greaney M.L., Nigg C.R., Lees F.D., Burbank P.M. and Clark P.G. Physical activity, physical function, and stages of change in older adults. *Am J Health Behav.* 2005: 29(1): 70-80.

163 Roessler, K. (2002). *Når idræt gør ondt - skader, smerter, stress.* Århus: Forlaget Klim.

164 Roessler K.K. & Ibsen B. Promoting exercise on prescription: recruitment, motivation, barriers and adherence in a Danish community intervention study to reduce type 2 diabetes, dyslipidemia and hypertension. *J Public Health.* 2009: 17(1).

165 Roessler, K. K., Ibsen, B, Saltin, B., and Sørensen, J. (2007). *Fysisk aktivitet som behandling - Motion og Kost på Recept i Københavns Kommune* Odense: Syddansk Universitetsforlag.

166 Sallis J.F., Haskell W.L., Fortmann S.P., Vranizan K.M., Taylor C.B. and Solomon D.S. Predictors of adoption and maintenance of physical activity in a community sample. *Prev Med.* 1986: 15(4): 331-341.

167 Sallis J.F. & Hovell M.F. Determinants of exercise behavior. *Exerc Sport Sci Rev.* 1990: 18: 307-330.

168 Sallis J.F., Hovell M.F., Hofstetter C.R., Faucher P., Elder J.P., Blanchard J., Caspersen C.J., Powell K.E. and Christenson G.M. A multivariate study of determinants of vigorous exercise in a community sample. *Prev Med.* 1989: 18(1): 20-34.

169 Sarkin J.A., Johnson S.S., Prochaska J.O. and Prochaska J.M. Applying the transtheoretical model to regular moderate exercise in an overweight population: validation of a stages of change measure. *Prev Med.* 2001: 33(5): 462-469.

170 Schein E.H. Kurt Lewin´s Change Theory in the Field and in the Classroom: Notes Toward a Model of Managed Learning. *The SoL Journal, on Knowlegde, Learning and Change.* MIT Press. 2006: 1(1): 59-72.

171 Schumann A., Estabrooks P.A., Nigg C.R. and Hill J. Validation of the stages of change with mild, moderate, and strenuous physical activity behavior, intentions, and self-efficacy. *Int J Sports Med.* 2003: 24(5): 363-365.

172 Schumann A., Nigg C.R., Rossi J.S., Jordan P.J., Norman G.J., Garber C.E., Riebe D. and Benisovich S.V. Construct validity of the stages of change of exercise adoption for different intensities of physical activity in four samples of differing age groups. *Am J Health Promot.* 2002: 16(5): 280-287.

173 Schutzer K.A. & Graves B.S. Barriers and motivations to exercise in older adults. *Prev Med.* 2004: 39(5): 1056-1061.

174 Schwarzer, R. (1992). Self-efficacy in the adoption and maintenance of health behaviors: Theoretical approaches and a new model. In Schwarzer, R., *Self-efficacy: thought control of action* (217-243). Washington: Hemisphere Publishing Corporation.

175 Shao J. & Zhong B. Last observation carry-forward and last observation analysis. *Stat Med.* 2003: 22(15): 2429-2441.

176 Shephard R.J. Limits to the measurement of habitual physical activity by questionnaires. *Br J Sports Med.* 2003: 37(3): 197-206.

177 Sherwood N.E., Martinson B.C., Crain A.L., Hayes M.G., Pronk N.P. and O'Connor P.J. A new approach to physical activity maintenance: rationale, design, and baseline data from the Keep Active Minnesota Trial. *BMC Geriatr.* 2008: 8: 17.

178 Singer, J. and Willet, J. (2003). *Applied Longitudinal Data Analysis. Modeling Change and Event Occurence.* Oxford: Oxford University Press.

179 Sjostrand L. Galenos-the most influential physician in medical history. Medicine for him was a universal science. *Lakartidningen*. 2002: 99(47): 4752-4754.

180 Skovgaard, T. (2004). Fysisk aktivitet som sundhedsadfærd. In Lüders, K. and Vogensen, N., *Idrætspædagogisk Årbog 2004 / 05* (13-44). Slagelse: Bavnebanke.

181 Skovgaard T, Sorensen J.B., Sørensen J., Bredahl T.V. and Puggaard L. Motion på recept: syddanske erfaringer. *Månedsskr prakt lægeg*. 2009.

182 Sørensen, J. (2008). *The effect of intervention with "Exercise on Prescription" on physical activity, fitnes and health in sedentary patients with lifestyle diseases*. University of Southern Denmark, Odense.

183 Sørensen J., Sørensen J.B., Skovgaard T., Bredahl T.V.G. and Puggaard L. Exercise on Prescription: Changes in physical activity and health-related quality of life in five Danish programmes. *Eur J Public Health*. 2010. doi:10.1093/eurpub/ckq003

184 Sorensen J.B., Kragstrup J., Kjaer K. and Puggaard L. Exercise on prescription: trial protocol and evaluation of outcomes. *BMC Health Serv Res*. 2007: 7: 36.

185 Sorensen J.B., Kragstrup J., Skovgaard T. and Puggaard L. Exercise on prescription: a randomized study on the effect of counseling vs counseling and supervised exercise. *Scand J Med Sci Sports*. 2008: 18(3): 288-297.

186 Sorensen J.B., Skovgaard T. and Puggaard L. Exercise on prescription in general practice: A systematic review. *Scand J Prim Health Care*. 2006: 24(2): 69-74.

187 Staten L.K., Taren D.L., Howell W.H., Tobar M., Poehlman E.T., Hill A., Reid P.M. and Ritenbaugh C. Validation of the Arizona Activity Frequency Questionnaire using doubly labeled water. *Med Sci Sports Exerc*. 2001: 33(11): 1959-1967.

188 Statens Institut for Folkesundhed (2006). *Sundheds- og sygelighedsundersøgelsen 2005. Interviewskema med svarfordeling*. København: Statens Institut for Folkesundhed.

189 Steptoe A., Rink E. and Kerry S. Psychosocial predictors of changes in physical activity in overweight sedentary adults following counseling in primary care. *Prev Med*. 2000: 31(2 Pt 1): 183-194.

190 Stroebe, W. (2000). *Social psychology and health*. (2. ed. ed.) Philadelphia, PA: Open University Press.

191 Sundhedsstyrelsen (2004). *Fysisk Aktivitet - håndbog om forebyggelse og behandling* (Rep. No. 1). København: Sundhedsstyrelsen.

192 Sundhedsstyrelsen (2006). *Fysisk Aktivitet og Evidens - Livsstilssygdomme, folkesygdomme og risikofaktorer mv. Et opslagsværk til rådgivning og pressedækning* København: Sundhedsstyrelsen.

193 Sutton, S. (2004). Determinants of health-related behaviors: Theoretical and methodological issues. In Sutton, S., Baum, A., and Johnston, M., *The SAGE Handbook of Health Psychology* (94-126). London: SAGE.

References

194 Suzuki I. Reliability and Validity of a Questionaire for Assessment of Energy Expenditure and Physical Activity in Epidemiological Studies. *Journal of Epidemiology*. 1998: 8(3 Aug): 152-159.

195 Taylor A.H. & Fox K.R. Effectiveness of a primary care exercise referral intervention for changing physical self-perceptions over 9 months. *Health Psychol*. 2005: 24(1): 11-21.

196 Thing L.F. Motion på recept - er en svær pille at sluge! En sociologisk diskussion af motion som behandling i velfærdsstaten. 2005. *www.idrottsforum.org*.

197 Thing L.F. Motion på recept - er en svær pille at sluge! Månedsskr prakt lægeg. Kbh.: *Månedsskrift for Praktisk Lægegerning*. 2007: 85(2): 219-224.

198 Tinetti M.E. & Fried T. The end of the disease era. *Am J Med*. 2004: 116(3): 179-185.

199 Trost S.G., Owen N., Bauman A.E., Sallis J.F. and Brown W. Correlates of adults' participation in physical activity: review and update. *Med Sci Sports Exerc*. 2002: 34(12): 1996-2001.

200 Tuomilehto J., Lindstrom J., Eriksson J.G., Valle T.T., Hamalainen H., Ilanne-Parikka P., Keinanen-Kiukaanniemi S., Laakso M., Louheranta A., Rastas M., Salminen V. and Uusitupa M. Prevention of type 2 diabetes mellitus by changes in lifestyle among subjects with impaired glucose tolerance. *N Engl J Med*. 2001: 344(18): 1343-1350.

201 Uchino B.N., Cacioppo J.T. and Kiecolt-Glaser J.K. The relationship between social support and physiological processes: a review with emphasis on underlying mechanisms and implications for health. *Psychol Bull*. 1996: 119(3): 488-531.

202 Uexküll, T. V. (1996). *Psychosomatische Medizin*. München: Urban & Schwarzenberg.

203 Vallerand, R. J. (2007). A Hierarchical Model of Intrinsic and Extrinsic Motivation for Sport and Physical Activity. In Hagger, M. S. and Chatzisarantis, N. L. D., *Intrinsic Motivation and Self-Determination in Exercise and Sport* (255-279). Champaign, IL: Human Kinetics.

204 van Sluijs, E. M. (2004). *Effectiveness of physical activity promotion: The case of general practice*. VU University Medical Center Amsterdam, Wageningen, NL.

205 van Sluijs E.M., van Poppel M.N., Twisk J.W., Brug J. and van M.W. The positive effect on determinants of physical activity of a tailored, general practice-based physical activity intervention. *Health Educ Res*. 2005a: 20(3): 345-356.

206 van Sluijs E.M., van Poppel M.N., Twisk J.W., Chin A.P.M., Calfas K.J and van M.W. Effect of a tailored physical activity intervention delivered in general practice settings: results of a randomized controlled trial. *Am J Public Health*. 2005b: 95(10): 1825-1831.

207 van Sluijs E.M., van Poppel M.N. and van M.W. Stage-based lifestyle interventions in primary care: are they effective? *Am J Prev Med*. 2004: 26(4): 330-343.

208 VanLeeuwen J.A., Waltner-Toews D., Abernathy T. and Smit B. Evolving models of human health toward an ecosystem context. *Ecosystem Health*. 1999: 5(3): 204-219.

209   Verbeke, G. and Molenberghs, G. (2000). *Linear mixed models for longitudinal data*. New York: Springer.

210   Wareham N.J. & Rennie K.L. The assessment of physical activity in individuals and populations: why try to be more precise about how physical activity is assessed? *Int J Obes Relat Metab Disord*. 1998: 22 Suppl 2: S30-S38.

211   Webster C. Paracelsus, and 500 years of encouraging scientific inquiry. *BMJ*. 1993: 306(6878): 597-598.

212   Whelton S.P., Chin A., Xin X. and He J. Effect of aerobic exercise on blood pressure: a meta-analysis of randomized, controlled trials. *Ann Intern Med*. 2002: 136(7): 493-503.

213   White, P. (2005). *Biopsychosocial medicine: an integrated approach to understanding illness*. Oxford: Oxford University Press.

214   WHO (1948). *Constitution of the World Health Organisation* Geneva: WHO.

215   WHO (2004). *Global strategy on diet, physical activity and health* France: WHO.

216   WHO (22-7-2009). WHO definition of Health. WHO [On-line]. Available: http://www.who.int/about/definition/en/print.html.

217   WHO/FAO (2003). *Diet, nutrition and the prevention of chronic diseases* (Volume 916). Geneva, Switzerland: WHO.

218   Willeman, M. (2004). *Motion på recept - en litteraturgennemgang med fokus på effekter og organisering* (Rep. No. -). København: Viden- og dokumentationsenheden, Sundhedsstyrelsen.

219   Winau, R. (1990). Sygdomsbegreb og Kropsbegreb - i den vestlige medicin. In Jespersen, E, *Centring* (25 ed., 57-67). Slagelse: Forlaget Bavnebanke.

220   Yalom, I. D. (1985). *The theory and practice of group psychotherapy*. (3 ed.) New York: Basic Books.

221   Yancey A.K., Wold C.M., McCarthy W.J., Weber M.D., Lee B., Simon P.A. and Fielding J.E. Physical inactivity and overweight among Los Angeles County adults. *Am J Prev Med*. 2004: 27(2): 146-152.

222   Zachariae B. Evidensbaseret psykologisk praksis. Psykolog Nyt. *Dansk Psykolog Forening*. 2007:(12): 16-25.

223   Zachariae, R. (1996). *Mind and Immunity. Psychological modulation of immunological and inflammatory parameters*. København: Munksgaard.

2148842R00074

Printed in Great Britain
by Amazon.co.uk, Ltd.,
Marston Gate.

90 0506888 8

Continental Reactivation and Reworking

Special Publication reviewing procedures

The Society makes every effort to ensure that the scientific and production quality of its books matches that of its journals. Since 1997, all book proposals have been refereed by specialist reviewers as well as by the Society's Publications Committee. If the referees identify weaknesses in the proposal, these must be addressed before the proposal is accepted.

Once the book is accepted, the Society has a team of series editors (listed above) who ensure that the volume editors follow strict guidelines on refereeing and quality control. We insist that individual papers can only be accepted after satisfactory review by two independent referees. The questions on the review forms are similar to those for *Journal of the Geological Society*. The referees' forms and comments must be available to the Society's series editors on request.

Although many of the books result from meetings, the editors are expected to commission papers that were not presented at the meeting to ensure that the book provides a balanced coverage of the subject. Being accepted for presentation at the meeting does not guarantee inclusion in the book.

Geological Society Special Publications are included in the ISI Science Citation Index, but they do not have an impact factor, the latter being applicable only to journals.

More information about submitting a proposal and producing a Special Publication can be found on the Society's web site: www.geolsoc.org.uk.